JUVENILE
AND MINOR POEMS,

BY

Robert Southey.

In Two Volumes.

VOL. II.

Painted by T. Creswick.   Engraved by E. Finden.

The Summer Bower.

Derwent Island.

LONDON.
LONGMAN, BROWN, GREEN AND LONGMANS,
PATERNOSTER ROW.

Drawn by J. Creswick.   Engraved by E. Finden.

VIEW OF KESWICK, SKIDDAW, AND M.ʳ SOUTHEY'S HOUSE.

London Longman & Cº

THE

POETICAL WORKS

OF

ROBERT SOUTHEY,

COLLECTED BY HIMSELF.

IN TEN VOLUMES.

VOL. III.

LONDON:

LONGMAN, BROWN, GREEN, AND LONGMANS.

PATERNOSTER-ROW.

JUVENILE AND MINOR POEMS.

VOL. II.

Que fol ou que sage on m'estime,
Et que je sois Poete ou non,
Toutefois si j'aime la rime,
J'aime beaucoup mieux la raison.

JEAN DU NESME.

CONTENTS.

A 4

Page

CONTENTS.

PREFACE.

In a former Preface my obligations to Akenside
were acknowledged, with especial reference to the
Hymn to the Penates ; the earliest of my Inscrip-
tions also originated in the pleasure with which
I perused those of this favourite author. Others
of a later date bear a nearer resemblance to the
general character of Chiabrera's epitaphs. Those
which relate to the Peninsular War are part of a
series which I once hoped to have completed. The
epitaph for Bishop Butler was originally composed
in the lapidary style, to suit the monument in
Bristol Cathedral : it has been remodelled here,
that I might express myself more at length, and
in a style more accordant with my own judgement.

One thing remains to be explained, and I shall
then have said all that it becomes me to say concerning these Minor Poems.

It was stated in some of the newspapers that Walter
Scott and myself became competitors for the Poet-
Laureateship upon the death of Mr. Pye ; that we
met accidentally at the Prince Regent's levee, each

in pursuit of his pretensions, and that some words
which were not over-courteous on either side passed
between us on the occasion;—to such impudent
fabrications will those persons resort who make it
their business to pander for public curiosity.   The
circumstances relating to that appointment have
been made known in Mr. Lockhart's Life of Sir
Walter.   His conduct was, as it always was, cha-
racteristically generous, and in the highest degree
friendly.   Indeed, it was neither in his nature nor
in mine to place ourselves in competition with
any one, or ever to regard a contemporary as a
rival.   The world was wide enough for us all.

Upon his declining the office, and using his
influence, without my knowledge, to obtain it for
me, his biographer says*, " Mr. Southey was in-
vited to accept the vacant laurel ; and to the honour
of the Prince Regent, when he signified that his
acceptance must depend on the office being thenceforth so modified as to demand none of the old
formal odes, leaving it to the Poet-Laureate to
choose his own time for celebrating any great public
event that might occur, his Royal Highness had
the good sense and good taste at once to acquiesce
in the propriety of this alteration.   The office was
thus relieved from the burden of ridicule which
had, in spite of so many illustrious names, adhered

* Vol. iii. p. 88.

to it." The alteration, however, was not brought about exactly in this manner.

I was on the way to London when the correspondence upon this subject between Sir Walter Scott and Mr. Croker took place : a letter from Scott followed me thither, and on my arrival in town I was informed of what had been done. No wish for the Laureateship had passed across my mind, nor had I ever dreamt that it would be proposed to me. My first impulse was to decline it; not from any fear of ridicule, still less of obloquy, but because I had ceased for several years to write occasional verses : the inclination had departed; and though willing as a bee to work from morn till night in collecting honey, I had a great dislike to spinning like a spider. Other considerations overcame this reluctance, and made it my duty to accept the appointment. I then expressed a wish to Mr. Croker that it might be placed upon a footing which would exact from the holder nothing like a schoolboy's task, but leave him at liberty to write when, and in what manner, he thought best, and thus render the office as honourable as it was originally designed to be. Upon this, Mr. Croker, whose friendliness to me upon every occasion I gladly take this opportunity of acknowledging, observed that it was not for us to make terms with the Prince Regent. "Go you," said he, " and write your Ode for the New Year.

You can never have a better subject than the
present state of the war affords you." He added
that some fit time might be found for representing
the matter to the Prince in its proper light.

My appointment had no sooner been made known,
than I received a note with Sir William Parsons's
compliments, requesting that I would let him have
the Ode as soon as possible, Mr. Pye having always
provided him with it six weeks before the New
Year's Day. I was not wanting in punctuality;
nevertheless, it was a great trouble to Sir William
that the office should have been conferred upon a
poet who did not walk in the ways of his prede-
cessor, and do according to all things that he had
done ; for Mr. Pye had written his odes always in
regular stanzas and in rhyme. Poor Sir William,
though he had not fallen upon evil tongues and
evil times, thought he had fallen upon evil ears
when he was to set verses like mine to music.

But the labour which the Chief Musician bestowed upon the verses of the Chief Poet was so
much labour lost. The performance of the Annual
Odes had been suspended from the time of the
King's illness, in 1810. Under the circumstances of
his malady, any festal celebration of the birth-day
would have been a violation of natural feeling and
public propriety. On those occasions it was certain
that nothing would be expected from me during the

life of George III. But the New Year's performance might perhaps be called for, and for that, therefore, I always prepared. Upon the accession of George IV. I made ready an Ode for St. George's Day, which Mr. Shield, who was much better satisfied with his yoke-fellow than Sir William had been, thought happily suited for his purpose. It was indeed well suited for us both. All my other Odes related to the circumstances of the passing times, and could have been appropriately performed only when they were composed; but this was a standing subject, and, till this should be called for, it was needless to provide anything else. The annual performance had, however, by this time fallen completely into disuse; and thus terminated a custom which may truly be said to have been more honoured in the breach than in the observance.

Keswick, Dec. 12. 1837.

ENGLISH ECLOGUES.

THE following Eclogues, I believe, bear no resemblance to any poems in our language. This species of composition has become popular in Germany, and I was induced to attempt it by what was told me of the German Idylls by my friend Mr. William Taylor of Norwich. So far, therefore, these pieces may be deemed imitations, though I am not acquainted with the German language at present, and have never seen any translations or specimens in this kind.

With bad Eclogues I am sufficiently acquainted, from Tityrus and Corydon down to our English Strephons and Thirsisses. No kind of poetry can boast of more illustrious names, or is more distinguished by the servile dulness of imitated nonsense. Pastoral writers, " more silly than their sheep," have, like their sheep, gone on in the same track one after another. Gay struck into a new path. His eclogues were the only ones which interested me when I was a boy, and did not know they were burlesque. The subject would furnish matter for an essay, but this is not the place for it.

1799.

I.

THE OLD MANSION-HOUSE.

STRANGER.

OLD friend! why you seem bent on parish duty,
Breaking the highway stones,.. and 't is a task
Somewhat too hard methinks for age like yours!

OLD MAN.

Why yes! for one with such a weight of years
Upon his back!.. I 've lived here, man and boy,
In this same parish, well nigh the full age
Of man, being hard upon threescore and ten.
I can remember sixty years ago
The beautifying of this mansion here,
When my late Lady's father, the old Squire,
Came to the estate.

STRANGER.

       Why then you have outlasted
All his improvements, for you see they 're making
Great alterations here.

OLD MAN.

       Aye .. great indeed!
And if my poor old Lady could rise up ..
God rest her soul! 't would grieve her to behold
What wicked work is here.

STRANGER.
                    They 've set about it
In right good earnest.   All the front is gone ;
Here 's to be turf, they tell me, and a road
Round to the door. There were some yew trees too
Stood in the court...

OLD MAN.
                    Aye, Master ! fine old trees !
Lord bless us ! I have heard my father say
His grandfather could just remember back
When they were planted there.   It was my task
To keep them trimm'd, and 't was a pleasure to me;
All straight and smooth, and like a great green wall !
My poor old lady many a time would come
And tell me where to clip, for she had play'd
In childhood under them, and 't was her pride
To keep them in their beauty.   Plague, I say,
On their new-fangled whimsies ! we shall have
A modern shrubbery here stuck full of firs
And your pert poplar trees ; ... I could as soon
Have plough'd my father's grave as cut them down !

STRANGER.
But 't will be lighter and more chearful now ;
A fine smooth turf, and with a carriage road
That sweeps conveniently from gate to gate.
I like a shrubbery too, for it looks fresh ;
And then there 's some variety about it.
In spring the lilac and the snow-ball flower,
And the laburnum with its golden strings
Waving in the wind : And when the autumn comes
The bright red berries of the mountain-ash,

With pines enough in winter to look green,
And show that something lives.   Sure this is better
Than a great hedge of yew, making it look
All the year round like winter, and for ever
Dropping its poisonous leaves from the under boughs
Wither'd and bare.

OLD MAN.

Aye! so the new Squire thinks;
And pretty work he makes of it!   What 't is
To have a stranger come to an old house!

STRANGER.

It seems you know him not?

OLD MAN.

No, Sir, not I.
They tell me he 's expected daily now;
But in my Lady's time he never came
But once, for they were very distant kin.
If he had play'd about here when a child
In that fore court, and eat the yew-berries,
And sate in the porch, threading the jessamine flowers
Which fell so thick, he had not had the heart
To mar all thus!

STRANGER.

Come.! come! all is not wrong;
Those old dark windows...

OLD MAN.

They 're demolish'd too,..
B 3

As if he could not see through casement glass!
The very red-breasts, that so regular
Came to my Lady for her morning crumbs,
Wo'n't know the windows now!

STRANGER.

                Nay they were small,
And then so darken'd round with jessamine,
Harbouring the vermin ; . . yet I could have wish'd
That jessamine had been saved, which canopied
And bower'd and lined the porch.

OLD MAN.

                It did one good
To pass within ten yards when 't was in blossom.
There was a sweet-briar too that grew beside ;
My Lady loved at evening to sit there
And knit ; and her old dog lay at her feet
And slept in the sun ; 't was an old favourite dog,..
She did not love him less that he was old
And feeble, and he always had a place
By the fire-side : and when he died at last
She made me dig a grave in the garden for him.
For she was good to all ! a woeful day
'T was for the poor when to her grave she went !

STRANGER.

They lost a friend then?

OLD MAN.

              You 're a stranger here,
Or you wouldn't ask that question. Were they sick ?

She had rare cordial waters, and for herbs
She could have taught the Doctors. Then at winter,
When weekly she distributed the bread
In the poor old porch, to see her and to hear
The blessings on her ! and I warrant them
They were a blessing to her when her wealth
Had been no comfort else.   At Christmas, Sir !
It would have warm'd your heart if you had seen
Her Christmas kitchen, .. how the blazing fire
Made her fine pewter shine, and holly boughs
So chearful red, ... and as for misseltoe, ..
The finest bush that grew in the country round
Was mark'd for Madam.   Then her old ale went
So bountiful about ! a Christmas cask,
And 't was a noble one ! ... God help me, Sir !
But I shall never see such days again.

STRANGER.

Things may be better yet than you suppose,
And you should hope the best.

OLD MAN.

                    It don't look well, ..
These alterations, Sir ! I 'm an old man,
And love the good old fashions ; we don't find
Old bounty in new houses. They 've destroy'd
All that my Lady loved ; her favourite walk
Grubb'd up, .. and they do say that the great row
Of elms behind the house, which meet a-top,
They must fall too.   Well ! well ! I did not think
To live to see all this, and 't is perhaps
A comfort I shan't live to see it long.

B 4

STRANGER.

But sure all changes are not needs for the worse,
My friend?

OLD MAN.

      May-hap they mayn't, Sir; .. for all that
I like what I 've been used to.   I remember
All this from a child up, and now to lose it,
'T is losing an old friend.   There 's nothing left
As 't was; .. I go abroad and only meet
With men whose fathers I remember boys ;
The brook that used to run before my door,
That 's gone to the great pond; the trees I learnt
To climb are down ; and I see nothing now
That tells me of old times, .. except the stones
In the churchyard.   You are young, Sir, and I hope
Have many years in store, ... but pray to God
You mayn't be left the last of all your friends.

STRANGER.

Well! well! you've one friend more than you 're
      aware of.
If the Squire's taste don't suit with yours, I warrant
That 's all you 'll quarrel with : walk in and taste
His beer, old friend! and see if your old Lady
E'er broach'd a better cask. You did not know me,
But we 're acquainted now.   'T would not be easy
To make you like the outside ; but within,
That is not changed, my friend! you 'll always find
The same old bounty and old welcome there.

Westbury, 1798.

9

II.

THE GRANDMOTHER'S TALE.

JANE.

HARRY! I'm tired of playing. We'll draw round
The fire, and Grandmamma perhaps will tell us
One of her stories.

HARRY.

Aye .. dear Grandmamma!
A pretty story! something dismal now;
A bloody murder.

JANE.

Or about a ghost.

GRANDMOTHER.

Nay, nay, I should but frighten ye. You know
The other night when I was telling ye
About the light in the churchyard, how you trembled
Because the screech-owl hooted at the window,
And would not go to bed.

JANE.

Why, Grandmamma,
You said yourself you did not like to hear him.
Pray now! .. we wo'n't be frightened.

GRANDMOTHER.

Well, well, children!

But you 've heard all my stories... Let me see,...
Did I never tell you how the smuggler murder'd
The woman down at Pill?

HARRY.

No .. never ! never !

GRANDMOTHER.

Not how he cut her head off in the stable?

HARRY.

Oh ... now ! ... do tell us that !

GRANDMOTHER.

You must have heard
Your mother, children ! often tell of her.
She used to weed in the garden here, and worm
Your uncle's dogs*, and serve the house with coal;
And glad enough she was in winter time
To drive her asses here ! It was cold work
To follow the slow beasts through sleet and snow ;
And here she found a comfortable meal
And a brave fire to thaw her, for poor Moll
Was always welcome.

HARRY.

Oh ! 't was blear-eyed Moll
The collier woman,.. a great ugly woman ;
I 've heard of her.

---

* I know not whether this cruel and stupid custom is common in other parts of England. It is supposed to prevent the
dogs from doing any mischief, should they afterwards become
mad.

GRANDMOTHER.

Ugly enough, poor soul !
At ten yards' distance you could hardly tell
If it were man or woman, for her voice
Was rough as our old mastiff's, and she wore
A man's old coat and hat :.. and then her face !
There was a merry story told of her,
How when the press-gang came to take her husband
As they were both in bed, she heard them coming,
Drest John up in her night-cap, and herself
Put on his clothes and went before the captain.

JANE.

And so they prest a woman !

GRANDMOTHER.

'T was a trick
She dearly loved to tell ; and all the country
Soon knew the jest, for she was used to travel
For miles around.   All weathers and all hours
She cross'd the hill, as hardy as her beasts,
Bearing the wind and rain and drifting snow.
And if she did not reach her home at night,
She laid her down in the stable with her asses,
And slept as sound as they did.

HARRY.

With her asses !

GRANDMOTHER.

Yes ; and she loved her beasts. For though, poor wretch,
She was a terrible reprobate, and swore

Like any trooper, she was always good
To the dumb creatures ; never loaded them
Beyond their strength ; and rather, I believe,
Would stint herself than let the poor beasts want,
Because, she said, they could not ask for food.
I never saw her stick fall heavier on them
Than just with its own weight.   She little thought
This tender-heartedness would cause her death !
There was a fellow who had oftentimes,
As if he took delight in cruelty,
Ill-used her beasts.   He was a man who lived
By smuggling, and, .. for she had often met him,
Crossing the down at night, .. she threaten'd him,
If ever he abused them more, to inform
Of his unlawful ways.   Well .. so it was ..
'T was what they both were born to ! he provoked her :
She laid an information ; and one morning
They found her in the stable, her throat cut
From ear to ear, till the head only hung
Just by a bit of skin.

JANE.
Oh dear ! oh dear !

HARRY.
I hope they hung the man !

GRANDMOTHER.
They took him up ;
There was no proof, no one had seen the deed,
And he was set at liberty.   But God,
Whose eye beholdeth all things, He had seen

The murder ; and the murderer knew that God
Was witness to his crime.   He fled the place, ..
But nowhere could he fly the avenging hand
Of Heaven,..but nowhere could the murderer rest;..
A guilty conscience haunted him ; by day,
By night, in company, in solitude,
Restless and wretched, did he bear upon him
The weight of blood.   Her cries were in his ears ;
Her stifled groans, as when he knelt upon her,
Always he heard ; always he saw her stand
Before his eyes ; even in the dead of night
Distinctly seen as though in the broad sun,
She stood beside the murderer's bed, and yawn'd
Her ghastly wound ; till life itself became
A punishment at last he could not bear,
And he confess'd it all, and gave himself
To death ; so terrible, he said, it was
To have a guilty conscience !

HARRY.

Was he hung, then ?

GRANDMOTHER.

Hung and anatomized.   Poor wretched man,
Your uncles went to see him on his trial ;
He was so pale, so thin, so hollow-eyed,
And such a horror in his meagre face,
They said he look'd like one who never slept.
He begg'd the prayers of all who saw his end,
And met his death with fears that well might warn
From guilt, though not without a hope in Christ.

Westbury, 1798.

III.

HANNAH.

PASSING across a green and lonely lane
A funeral met our view. It was not here
A sight of every day, as in the streets
Of some great city, and we stopt and ask'd
Whom they were bearing to the grave. A girl,
They answer'd, of the village, who had pined
Through the long course of eighteen painful months
With such slow wasting, that the hour of death
Came welcome to her. We pursued our way
To the house of mirth, and with that idle talk
Which passes o'er the mind and is forgot,
We wore away the time. But it was eve
When homewardly I went, and in the air
Was that cool freshness, that discolouring shade
Which makes the eye turn inward : hearing then
Over the vale the heavy toll of death
Sound slow, it made me think upon the dead ;
I question'd more, and learnt her mournful tale.

　　She bore unhusbanded a mother's pains,
And he who should have cherish'd her, far off
Sail'd on the seas. Left thus, a wretched one,
Scorn made a mock of her, and evil tongues
Were busy with her name. She had to bear
The sharper sorrow of neglect from him
Whom she had loved too dearly. Once he wrote
But only once that drop of comfort came
To mingle with her cup of wretchedness ;

And when his parents had some tidings from him,
There was no mention of poor Hannah there,
Or 't was the cold enquiry, more unkind
Than silence. So she pined and pined away,
And for herself and baby toil'd and toil'd ;
Nor did she, even on her death-bed, rest
From labour, knitting there with lifted arms,
Till she sunk with very weakness. Her old mother
Omitted no kind office, working for her,
Albeit her hardest labour barely earn'd
Enough to keep life struggling, and prolong
The pains of grief and sickness. Thus she lay
On the sick bed of poverty, worn out
With her long suffering and those painful thoughts
Which at her heart were rankling, and so weak,
That she could make no effort to express
Affection for her infant ; and the child,
Whose lisping love perhaps had solaced her,
Shunn'd her as one indifferent. But she too
Had grown indifferent to all things of earth,
Finding her only comfort in the thought
Of that cold bed wherein the wretched rest.
There had she now, in that last home, been laid,
And all was over now, .. sickness and grief,
Her shame, her suffering, and her penitence, ..
Their work was done. The school-boys as they sport
In the churchyard, for awhile might turn away
From the fresh grave till grass should cover it ;
Nature would do that office soon ; and none
Who trod upon the senseless turf would think
Of what a world of woes lay buried there !

Burton, near Christ Church, 1797.

IV.

THE SAILOR'S MOTHER.

WOMAN.

SIR, for the love of God, some small relief
To a poor woman!

TRAVELLER.

                        Whither are you bound?
'T is a late hour to travel o'er these downs,
No house for miles around us, and the way
Dreary and wild.   The evening wind already
Makes one's teeth chatter; and the very Sun,
Setting so pale behind those thin white clouds,
Looks cold.   'T will be a bitter night!

WOMAN.

                                    Aye, Sir,
'T is cutting keen! I smart at every breath;
Heaven knows how I shall reach my journey's end,
For the way is long before me, and my feet,
God help me! sore with travelling. I would gladly,
If it pleased God, at once lie down and die.

TRAVELLER.

Nay, nay, cheer up! a little food and rest
Will comfort you; and then your journey's end
May make amends for all.   You shake your head,

And weep. Is it some mournful business then
That leads you from your home?

WOMAN.

Sir, I am going

To see my son at Plymouth, sadly hurt
In the late action, and in the hospital
Dying, I fear me, now.

TRAVELLER.

Perhaps your fears

Make evil worse. Even if a limb be lost,
There may be still enough for comfort left ;
An arm or leg shot off, there 's yet the heart
To keep life warm, and he may live to talk
With pleasure of the glorious fight that maim'd him,
Proud of his loss. Old England's gratitude
Makes the maim'd Sailor happy.

WOMAN.

'T is not that, . .

An arm or leg . . . I could have borne with that.
It was no ball, Sir, but some cursed thing
Which bursts * and burns that hurt him. Something,
   Sir,

---

* The stink-pots used on board the French ships. In the
engagement between the Mars and L'Hercule, some of our
sailors were shockingly mangled by them : one, in particular
as described in the Eclogue, lost both his eyes   It would be
right and humane to employ means of destruction, could the

They do not use on board our English ships,
It is so wicked !

TRAVELLER.

Rascals ! a mean art
Of cruel cowardice, yet all in vain !

WOMAN.

Yes, Sir ! and they should show no mercy to them
For making use of such unchristian arms.
I had a letter from the hospital,
He got some friend to write it, and he tells me
That my poor boy has lost his precious eyes,
Burnt out. Alas ! that I should ever live
To see this wretched day ! ... They tell me, Sir,
There is no cure for wounds like his. Indeed
'T is a hard journey that I go upon
To such a dismal end !

TRAVELLER.

He yet may live.
But if the worst should chance, why you must bear
The will of Heaven with patience. Were it not
Some comfort to reflect your son has fallen
Fighting his country's cause ? and for yourself
You will not in unpitied poverty
Be left to mourn his loss. Your grateful country,
Amid the triumph of her victory,

---

be discovered, powerful enough to destroy fleets and armies;
but to use any thing that only inflicts additional torture upon
the sufferers in war, is altogether wicked.

Remembers those who paid its price of blood,
And with a noble charity relieves
The widow and the orphan.

WOMAN.

             God reward them!
God bless them!   It will help me in my age, ..
But, Sir! it will not pay me for my child!

TRAVELLER.

Was he your only child?

WOMAN.

             My only one,
The stay and comfort of my widowhood,
A dear good boy!.. When first he went to sea
I felt what it would come to,.. something told me
I should be childless soon.   But tell me, Sir,
If it be true that for a hurt like his
There is no cure? Please God to spare his life
Though he be blind, yet I should be so thankful!
I can remember there was a blind man
Lived in our village, one from his youth up
Quite dark, and yet he was a merry man,
And he had none to tend on him so well
As I would tend my boy!

TRAVELLER.

             Of this be sure,
His hurts are look'd to well, and the best help
The land affords, as rightly is his due,
Ever at hand.   How happen'd it he left you?
Was a seafaring life his early choice?

WOMAN.

No, Sir! poor fellow,.. he was wise enough
To be content at home, and 't was a home
As comfortable, Sir! even though I say it,
As any in the country.   He was left
A little boy when his poor father died,
Just old enough to totter by himself,
And call his mother's name.   We two were all,
And as we were not left quite destitute,
We bore up well.   In the summer time I work'd
Sometimes a-field.   Then I was famed for knitting,
And in long winter nights my spinning wheel
Seldom stood still.   We had kind neighbours too,
And never felt distress.   So he grew up
A comely lad, and wonderous well disposed ;
I taught him well ; there was not in the parish
A child who said his prayers more regular,
Or answered readier through his Catechism.
If I had foreseen this ! but 't is a blessing
We don't know what we 're born to !

TRAVELLER.

                      But how came it
He chose to be a Sailor ?

WOMAN.

                      You shall hear, Sir ;
As he grew up he used to watch the birds
In the corn, child's work you know, and easily done.
'T is an idle sort of task ; so he built up
A little hut of wicker-work and clay
Under the hedge, to shelter him in rain :

And then he took, for very idleness,
To making traps to catch the plunderers;
All sorts of cunning traps that boys can make,..
Propping a stone to fall and shut them in,
Or crush them with its weight, or else a springe
Swung on a bough. He made them cleverly,..
And, I, poor foolish woman! I was pleased
To see the boy so handy. You may guess
What follow'd, Sir, from this unlucky skill.
He did what he should not when he was older:
I warn'd him oft enough; but he was caught
In wiring hares at last, and had his choice,
The prison or the ship.

TRAVELLER.

The choice at least
Was kindly left him; and for broken laws
This was, methinks, no heavy punishment.

WOMAN.

So I was told, Sir. And I tried to think so,
But 't was a sad blow to me! I was used
To sleep at nights as sweetly as a child, ..
Now if the wind blew rough, it made me start,
And think of my poor boy tossing about
Upon the roaring seas. And then I seem'd
To feel that it was hard to take him from me
For such a little fault. But he was wrong,
Oh very wrong, .. a murrain on his traps!
See what they 've brought him to!

c 3

TRAVELLER.

                    Well! well! take comfort
He will be taken care of if he lives;
And should you lose your child, this is a country
Where the brave Sailor never leaves a parent
To weep for him in want.

WOMAN.

                    Sir, I shall want
No succour long.   In the common course of years
I soon must be at rest; and 't is a comfort,
When grief is hard upon me, to reflect
It only leads me to that rest the sooner.

Westbury, 1798.

V.

THE WITCH.

FATHER! here, father! I have found a horse-shoe!
Faith it was just in time; for t' other night
I laid two straws across at Margery's door,
And ever since I fear'd that she might do me
A mischief for 't. There was the Miller's boy
Who set his dog at that black cat of hers, ..
I met him upon crutches, and he told me
'T was all her evil eye.

          'T is rare good luck!
I would have gladly given a crown for one
If 't would have done as well. But where didst find it?

Down on the common; I was going a-field,
And neighbour Saunders pass'd me on his mare;
He had hardly said "Good day," before I saw
The shoe drop off. 'T was just upon my tongue
To call him back; .. it makes no difference does it,
Because I know whose 't was?

FATHER.

Why no, it can 't.
The shoe's the same, you know; and you did find it.

NATHANIEL.

That mare of his has got a plaguey road
To travel, father; .. and if he should lame her, ..
For she is but tender-footed, ..

FATHER.

Ay, indeed ! .
I should not like to see her limping back,
Poor beast ! .. But charity begins at home,
And, Nat, there's our own horse in such a way
This morning !

NATHANIEL.

Why he han't been rid again !
Last night I hung a pebble by the manger
With a hole through, and every body says
That 't is a special charm against the hags.

FATHER.

It could not be a proper natural hole then,
Or 't was not a right pebble ; .. for I found him
Smoking with sweat, quaking in every limb,
And panting so !   Lord knows where he had been
When we were all asleep, through bush and brake,
Up-hill and down-hill all alike, full stretch
At such a deadly rate ! ..

NATHANIEL.

By land and water,

Over the sea, perhaps !.. I have heard tell
'T is many thousand miles off at the end
Of the world, where witches go to meet the Devil.
They used to ride on broomsticks, and to smear
Some ointment over them, and then away
Out at the window ! but 't is worse than all
To worry the poor beasts so.   Shame upon it
That in a Christian country they should let
Such creatures live!

FATHER.

        And when there's such plain proof!
I did but threaten her because she robb'd
Our hedge, and the next night there came a wind
That made me shake to hear it in my bed.
How came it that that storm unroof'd my barn,
And only mine in the parish?.. Look at her,
And that's enough ; she has it in her face !..
A pair of large dead eyes, sunk in her head,
Just like a corpse, and pursed with wrinkles round ;
A nose and chin that scarce leave room between
For her lean fingers to squeeze in the snuff ;
And when she speaks ! I 'd sooner hear a raven
Croak at my door !.. She sits there, nose and knees,
Smoke-dried and shrivell'd over a starved fire,
With that black cat beside her, whose great eyes
Shine like old Beelzebub's ; and to be sure
It must be one of his imps !.. Ay, nail it hard.

NATHANIEL.

I wish old Margery heard the hammer go !
She 'd curse the music !

FATHER.

              Here's the Curate coming,
He ought to rid the parish of such vermin!
In the old times they used to hunt them out,
And hang them without mercy; but, Lord bless us!
The world is grown so wicked!

CURATE.

              Good day, Farmer!
Nathaniel, what art nailing to the threshold?

NATHANIEL.

A horse-shoe, Sir; 't is good to keep off witchcraft,
And we're afraid of Margery.

CURATE.

              Poor old woman!
What can you fear from her?

FATHER.

              What can we fear?
Who lamed the Miller's boy? who raised the wind
That blew my old barn's roof down? who d' ye think
Rides my poor horse a' nights? who mocks the hounds?
But let me catch her at that trick again,
And I 've a silver bullet ready for her,
One that shall lame her, double how she will.

NATHANIEL.

What makes her sit there moping by herself.
With no soul near her but that great black cat?
And do but look at her!

CURATE.

Poor wretch; half blind
And crooked with her years, without a child
Or friend in her old age, 't is hard indeed
To have her very miseries made her crimes !
I met her but last week in that hard frost
Which made my young limbs ache, and when I ask'd
What brought her out in the snow, the poor old woman
Told me that she was forced to crawl abroad
And pick the hedges, just to keep herself
From perishing with cold, .. because no neighbour
Had pity on her age ; and then she cried,
And said the children pelted her with snow-balls,
And wish'd that she were dead

FATHER.

I wish she was !
She has plagued the parish long enough !

CURATE.

Shame, Farmer !
Is that the charity your Bible teaches ?

FATHER.

My Bible does not teach me to love witches.
I know what 's charity ; who pays his tithes
And poor-rates readier ?

CURATE.

Who can better do it ?
You 've been a prudent and industrious man,
And God has blest your labour.

FATHER.
                    Why, thank God, Sir,
I 've had no reason to complain of fortune.

CURATE.
Complain? why you are wealthy! All the parish
Look up to you.

FATHER.
                    Perhaps, Sir, I could tell
Guinea for guinea with the warmest of them.

CURATE.
You can afford a little to the poor;
And then, what 's better still, you have the heart
To give from your abundance.

FATHER.
                              God forbid
I should want charity!

CURATE.
                    Oh! 't is a comfort
To think at last of riches well employ'd!
I have been by a death-bed, and know the worth
Of a good deed at that most aweful hour
When riches profit not.
                        Farmer, I 'm going
To visit Margery. She is sick, I hear;..
Old, poor and sick! a miserable lot,
And death will be a blessing. You might send her
Some little matter, something comfortable,

That she may go down easier to the grave,
And bless you when she dies.

FATHER.

What ! is she going ?
Well God forgive her then, if she has dealt
In the black art !   I'll tell my dame of it,
And she shall send her something.

CURATE.

So I'll say ;
And take my thanks for hers.   [*Goes.*]

FATHER.

That's a good man
That Curate, Nat, of ours, to go and visit
The poor in sickness ; but he don't believe
In witchcraft, and that is not like a Christian.

NATHANIEL.

And so old Margery's dying !

FATHER.

But you know
She may recover : so drive 't other nail in.

Westbury, 1798.

VI.

THE RUINED COTTAGE.

Ay, Charles! I knew that this would fix thine eye ;..
This woodbine wreathing round the broken porch,
Its leaves just withering, yet one autumn flower
Still fresh and fragrant; and yon holly-hock
That through the creeping weeds and nettles tall
Peers taller, lifting, column-like, a stem
Bright with its roseate blossoms. I have seen
Many an old convent reverend in decay,
And many a time have trod the castle courts
And grass-green halls, yet never did they strike
Home to the heart such melancholy thoughts
As this poor cottage. Look! its little hatch
Fleeced with that grey and wintry moss; the roof
Part moulder'd in, the rest o'ergrown with weeds,
House-leek, and long thin grass, and greener moss :
So Nature steals on all the works of man,
Sure conqueror she, reclaiming to herself
His perishable piles.
                        I led thee here,
Charles, not without design; for this hath been
My favourite walk even since I was a boy;
And I remember, Charles, this ruin here,
The neatest comfortable dwelling-place !
That when I read in those dear books which first

Woke in my heart the love of poesy,
How with the villagers Erminia dwelt,
And Calidore for a fair shepherdess
Forsook his quest to learn the shepherd's lore,
My fancy drew from this the little hut
Where that poor princess wept her hopeless love,
Or where the gentle Calidore at eve
Led Pastorella home.   There was not then
A weed where all these nettles overtop
The garden-wall ; but sweet-briar, scenting sweet
The morning air ; rosemary and marjoram,
All wholesome herbs ; and then, that woodbine
        wreathed
So lavishly around the pillar'd porch
Its fragrant flowers, that when I past this way,
After a truant absence hastening home,
I could not chuse but pass with slacken'd speed
By that delightful fragrance.   Sadly changed
Is this poor cottage ! and its dwellers, Charles !..
Theirs is a simple melancholy tale, ..
There 's scarce a village but can fellow it :
And yet, methinks, it will not weary thee,
And should not be untold.

                    A widow here
Dwelt with an orphan grandchild : just removed
Above the reach of pinching poverty,
She lived on some small pittance which sufficed,
In better times, the needful calls of life,
Not without comfort.   I remember her
Sitting at evening in that open door-way,
And spinning in the sun.   Methinks I see her
Raising her eyes and dark-rimm'd spectacles

To see the passer-by, yet ceasing not
To twirl her lengthening thread : or in the garden,
On some dry summer evening, walking round
To view her flowers, and pointing as she lean'd
Upon the ivory handle of her stick,
To some carnation whose o'erheavy head
Needed support; while with the watering-pot
Joanna follow'd, and refresh'd and trimm'd
The drooping plant; Joanna, her dear child,
As lovely and as happy then as youth
And innocence could make her.
                              Charles, it seems
As though I were a boy again, and all
The mediate years with their vicissitudes
A half-forgotten dream.   I see the Maid
So comely in her Sunday dress ! her hair,
Her bright brown hair, wreathed in contracting curls;
And then her cheek ! it was a red and white
That made the delicate hues of art look loathsome.
The countrymen who on their way to church
Were leaning o'er the bridge, loitering to hear
The bell's last summons, and in idleness
Watching the stream below, would all look up
When she passed by. And her old Grandam, Charles,..
When I have heard some erring infidel
Speak of our faith as of a gloomy creed,
Inspiring superstitious wretchedness,
Her figure has recurr'd ; for she did love
The Sabbath-day ; and many a time hath cross'd
These fields in rain and through the winter snows,
When I, a graceless boy, and cold of foot,
Wishing the weary service at its end,

Have wonder'd wherefore that good dame came there,
Who, if it pleased her, might have staid beside
A comfortable fire.
                    One only care
Hung on her aged spirit.   For herself,
Her path was plain before her, and the close
Of her long journey near.   But then her child
Soon to be left alone in this bad world, ...
That was a thought which many a winter night
Had kept her sleepless ; and when prudent love
In something better than a servant's state
Had placed her well at last, it was a pang
Like parting life to part with her dear girl.

    One summer, Charles, when at the holidays
Return'd from school, I visited again
My old accustom'd walks, and found in them
A joy almost like meeting an old friend,
I saw the cottage empty, and the weeds
Already crowding the neglected flowers.
Joanna, by a villain's wiles seduced,
Had play'd the wanton, and that blow had reach'd
Her grandam's heart.   She did not suffer long ;
Her age was feeble, and this mortal grief
Brought her grey hairs with sorrow to the grave.

    I pass this ruin'd dwelling oftentimes,
And think of other days.   It wakes in me
A transient sadness ; but the feelings, Charles,
Which ever with these recollections rise,
I trust in God they will not pass away.
    Westbury, 1799.

VOL. III.   D

VII.

THE LAST OF THE FAMILY.

JAMES.

WHAT, Gregory, you are come, I see, to join us
On this sad business.

GREGORY.

              Aye, James, I am come,
But with a heavy heart, God knows it, man!
Where shall we meet the corpse?

JAMES.

              Some hour from hence;
By noon, and near about the elms, I take it.
This is not as it should be, Gregory,
Old men to follow young ones to the grave!
This morning when I heard the bell strike out,
I thought that I had never heard it toll
So dismally before.

GREGORY.

              Well, well! my friend,
'T is what we all must come to, soon or late.
But when a young man dies, in the prime of life,
One born so well, who might have blest us all
Many long years!..

JAMES.

             And then the family
Extinguish'd in him, and the good old name
Only to be remember'd on a tomb-stone!
A name that has gone down from sire to son
So many generations! ... Many a time
Poor master Edward, who is now a corpse,
When but a child, would come to me and lead me
To the great family-tree, and beg of me
To tell him stories of his ancestors,
Of Eustace, he that went to the Holy Land
With Richard Lion-heart, and that Sir Henry
Who fought at Cressy in King Edward's wars;
And then his little eyes would kindle so
To hear of their brave deeds! I used to think
The bravest of them all would not out-do
My darling boy.

GREGORY.

            This comes of your great schools
And college-breeding. Plague upon his guardians,
That would have made him wiser than his fathers!

JAMES.

If his poor father, Gregory, had but lived,
Things would not have been so. He, poor good man,
Had little of book-learning, but there lived not
A kinder, nobler-hearted gentleman,
One better to his tenants. When he died
There was not a dry eye for miles around.
Gregory, I thought that I could never know

A sadder day than that: but what was that,
Compared with this day's sorrow?

GREGORY.

                                        I remember,
Eight months ago, when the young Squire began
To alter the old mansion, they destroy'd
The martins' nests, that had stood undisturb'd
Under that roof,.. aye! long before my memory.
I shook my head at seeing it, and thought
No good could follow.

JAMES.

                        Poor young man! I loved him
Like my own child. I loved the family!
Come Candlemas, and I have been their servant
For five-and-forty years. I lived with them
When his good father brought my Lady home;
And when the young Squire was born, it did me good
To hear the bells so merrily announce
An heir.   This is indeed a heavy blow ...
I feel it, Gregory, heavier than the weigh
Of threescore years.   He was a noble lad,
I loved him dearly.

GREGORY.

                        Every body loved him.
Such a fine, generous, open-hearted Youth!
When he came home from school at holidays,
How I rejoiced to see him! He was sure
To come and ask of me what birds there were
About my fields; and when I found a covey,

There's not a testy Squire preserves his game
More charily, than I have kept them safe
For Master Edward.   And he look'd so well
Upon a fine sharp morning after them,
His brown hair frosted, and his cheek so flush'd
With such a wholesome ruddiness, .. ah, James,
But he was sadly changed when he came down
To keep his birth-day.

JAMES.

                        Changed ! why, Gregory,
'T was like a palsy to me, when he stepp'd
Out of the carriage.   He was grown so thin,
His cheek so delicate sallow, and his eyes
Had such a dim and rakish hollowness ;
And when he came to shake me by the hand,
And spoke as kindly to me as he used,
I hardly knew the voice.

GREGORY.

                        It struck a damp
On all our merriment.   'T was a noble Ox
That smoked before us, and the old October
Went merrily in everflowing cans ;
But 't was a skin-deep merriment.   My heart
Seem'd as it took no share.   And when we drank
His health, the thought came over me what cause
We had for wishing that, and spoilt the draught.
Poor Gentleman ! to think ten months ago
He came of age, and now !

D 3

JAMES.

I fear'd it then !

He look'd to me as one that was not long
For this world's business.

GREGORY.

When the Doctor sent him
Abroad to try the air, it made me certain
That all was over.   There's but little hope,
Methinks, that foreign parts can help a man
When his own mother-country will not do.
The last time he came down, these bells rung so
I thought they would have rock'd the old steeple down;
And now that dismal toll ! I would have staid
Beyond its reach, but this was a last duty :
I am an old tenant of the family,
Born on the estate, and now that I 've outlived it,
Why 't is but right to see it to the grave.
Have you heard aught of the new Squire ?

JAMES.

But little,
And that not well.   But be he what he may
Matters not much to me.   The love I bore
To the old family will not easily fix
Upon a stranger.   What's on the opposite hill ?
Is it not the funeral ?

GREGORY.

'T is, I think, some horsemen.
Aye ! there are the black cloaks ; and now I see
The white plumes on the hearse.

JAMES.

Between the trees; ..
'T is hid behind them now.

GREGORY.

Aye! now we see it,
And there 's the coaches following, we shall meet
About the bridge. Would that this day were over!
I wonder whose turn 's next.

JAMES.

God above knows.
When youth is summon'd what must age expect!
God make us ready, Gregory, when it comes!

Westbury, 1799.

VIII.

THE WEDDING.

TRAVELLER.

I PRAY you, wherefore are the village bells
Ringing so merrily?

WOMAN.

A wedding, Sir,..
Two of the village folk.   And they are right
To make a merry time on't while they may!
Come twelve-months hence, I warrant them they'd go
To church again more willingly than now.
If all might be undone.

TRAVELLER.

An ill-match'd pair,
So I conceive you.   Youth perhaps and age?

WOMAN.

No,..both are young enough.

TRAVELLER.

Perhaps the man then,
A lazy idler,..one who better likes
The alehouse than his work?

WOMAN.

                    Why, Sir, for that
He always was a well-condition'd lad,
One who 'd work hard and well ; and as for drink,
Save now and then mayhap at Christmas time,
Sober as wife could wish.

TRAVELLER.

                    Then is the girl
A shrew, or else untidy ; . . one to welcome
Her husband with a rude unruly tongue !
Or drive him from a foul and wretched home
To look elsewhere for comfort.   Is it so ?

WOMAN.

She 's notable enough ; and as for temper
The best good-humour'd girl !   You see yon house,
There by the aspen-tree, whose grey leaves shine
In the wind ? she lived a servant at the farm.
And often, as I came to weeding here,
I 've heard her singing as she milk'd her cows
So cheerfully, . . I did not like to hear her,
Because it made me think upon the days
When I had got as little on my mind,
And was as cheerful too.   But she would marry,
And folks must reap as they have sown. God help her !

TRAVELLER.

Why Mistress, if they both are well inclined,
Why should not both be happy ?

WOMAN.

                    They 've no money.

TRAVELLER.

But both can work; and sure as cheerfully
She'd labour for herself as at the farm.
And he wo' n't work the worse because he knows
That she will make his fire-side ready for him,
And watch for his return.

WOMAN.

All very well,
A little while.

TRAVELLER.

And what if they are poor?
Riches can't always purchase happiness;
And much we know will be expected there
Where much was given.

WOMAN.

All this I have heard at church!
And when I walk in the church-yard, or have been
By a death-bed, 't is mighty comforting.
But when I hear my children cry for hunger,
And see them shiver in their rags, .. God help me!
I pity those for whom these bells ring up
So merrily upon their wedding-day,
Because I think of mine.

TRAVELLER.

You have known trouble;
These haply may be happier.

WOMAN.

Why for that
I 've had my share; some sickness and some sorrow:

Well will it be for them to know no worse.
Yet I had rather hear a daughter's knell
Than her wedding-peal, Sir, if I thought her fate
Promised no better things.

TRAVELLER.

       Sure, sure, good woman,
You look upon the world with jaundiced eyes !
All have their cares; those who are poor want wealth,
They who have wealth want more ; so are we all
Dissatisfied, yet all live on, and each
Has his own comforts.

WOMAN.

       Sir ! d'ye see that horse
Turn'd out to common here by the way-side ?.
He 's high in bone, you may tell every rib
Even at this distance.   Mind him ! how he turns
His head, to drive away the flies that feed
On his gall'd shoulder !   There 's just grass enough
To disappoint his whetted appetite.
You see his *comforts*, Sir !

TRAVELLER.

       A wretched beast !
Hard labour and worse usage he endures
From some bad master.   But the lot of the poor
Is not like his.

WOMAN.

    In truth it is not, Sir !
For when the horse lies down at night, no cares
About to-morrow vex him in his dreams :

He knows no quarter-day, and when he gets
Some musty hay or patch of hedge-row grass,
He has no hungry children to claim part
Of his half meal !

TRAVELLER.

'T is idleness makes want,
And idle habits.   If the man will go
And spend his evenings by the alehouse fire,
Whom can he blame if there be want at home ?

WOMAN.

Aye ! idleness ! the rich folks never fail
To find some reason why the poor deserve
Their miseries ! .. Is it idleness, I pray you,
That brings the fever or the ague fit ?
That makes the sick one's sickly appetite
From dry bread and potatoes turn away ?
Is it idleness that makes small wages fail
For growing wants ? .. Six years agone, these bells
Rung on my wedding-day, and I was told
What I might look for, .. but I did not heed
Good counsel.   I had lived in service, Sir ;
Knew never what it was to want a meal ;
Lay down without one thought to keep me sleepless
Or trouble me in sleep ; had for a Sunday
My linen gown, and when the pedlar came
Could buy me a new ribbon. . . And my husband, . .
A towardly young man and well to do, . .
He had his silver buckles and his watch ;
There was not in the village one who look'd
Sprucer on holidays.   We married, Sir,

And we had children, but while wants increased
Wages stood still. The silver buckles went,
So went the watch; and when the holiday coat
Was worn to work, no new * one in its place.
For me .. you see my rags! but I deserve them,
For wilfully, like this new-married pair,
I went to my undoing.

TRAVELLER.

.But the parish ...

WOMAN.

Aye, it falls heavy there; and yet their pittance
Just serves to keep life in. A blessed prospect,
To slave while there is strength, in age the workhouse,
A parish shell at last, and the little bell
Toll'd hastily for a pauper's funeral!

TRAVELLER.

Is this your child?

WOMAN.

Aye, Sir; and were he drest

---

* A farmer once told the author of Malvern Hills, " that
he almost constantly remarked a gradation of changes in those
men he had been in the habit of employing. Young men,
he said, were generally neat in their appearance, active and
cheerful, till they became married and had a family, when
he had observed that their silver buttons, buckles, and watches
gradually disappeared, and their Sunday's clothes became
common without any other to supply their place, .. *but*, said
he, *some good comes from this, for they will then work for whatever they can get.*"

Note to COTTLE's Malvern Hills.

And clean'd, he'd be as fine a boy to look on
As the Squire's young master. These thin rags of his
Let comfortably in the summer wind ;
But when the winter comes, it pinches me
To see the little wretch ; I 've three besides ;
And, .. God forgive me ! but I often wish
To see them in their coffins. .. God reward you !
God bless you for your charity !

TRAVELLER.
You have taught me
To give sad meaning to the village bells !

Bristol, 1800.

IX.

THE ALDERMAN'S FUNERAL.

STRANGER.

WHOM are they ushering from the world, with all
This pageantry and long parade of death ?

TOWNSMAN.

A long parade, indeed, Sir, and yet here
You see but half; round yonder bend it reaches
A furlong further, carriage behind carriage.

STRANGER.

'T is but a mournful sight, and yet the pomp
Tempts me to stand a gazer.

TOWNSMAN.

             Yonder schoolboy
Who plays the truant, says the proclamation
Of peace was nothing to the show ; and even
The chairing of the members at election
Would not have been a finer sight than this ;
Only that red and green are prettier colours
Than all this mourning.   There, Sir, you behold
One of the red-gown'd worthies of the city,
The envy and the boast of our exchange ; . . .

Aye, what was worth, last week, a good half-million,
Screw'd down in yonder hearse!

STRANGER.

               Then he was born
Under a lucky planet, who to-day
Puts mourning on for his inheritance.

TOWNSMAN.

When first I heard his death, that very wish
Leapt to my lips; but now the closing scene
Of the comedy hath waken'd wiser thoughts;
And I bless God, that, when I go to the grave,
There will not be the weight of wealth like his
To sink me down.

STRANGER.

           The camel and the needle, ..
Is that then in your mind?

TOWNSMAN.

            Even so.   The text
Is Gospel-wisdom.   I would ride the camel, ...
Yea leap him flying, through the needle's eye,
As easily as such a pamper'd soul
Could pass the narrow gate.

STRANGER.

             Your pardon, Sir,
But sure this lack of Christian charity
Looks not like Christian truth.

TOWNSMAN.

Your pardon too, Sir,
If, with this text before me, I should feel
In the preaching mood! But for these barren fig-trees,
With all their flourish and their leafiness,
We have been told their destiny and use,
When the axe is laid unto the root, and they
Cumber the earth no longer.

STRANGER.

Was his wealth
Stored fraudfully, .. the spoil of orphans wrong'd,
And widows who had none to plead their right?

TOWNSMAN.

All honest, open, honourable gains,
Fair legal interest, bonds and mortgages,
Ships to the East and West.

STRANGER.

Why judge you then
So hardly of the dead?

TOWNSMAN.

For what he left
Undone; .. for sins, not one of which is written
In the Ten Commandments. He, I warrant him,
Believed no other Gods than those of the Creed;
Bow'd to no idols, .. but his money-bags;
Swore no false oaths, except at the custom-house;
Kept the Sabbath idle; built a monument
To honour his dead father; did no murder;

VOL. III.   E

Never sustain'd an action for crim-con ;
Never pick'd pockets ; never bore false-witness ;
And never, with that all-commanding wealth,
Coveted his neighbour's house, nor ox, nor ass !

STRANGER.

You knew him then it seems ?

TOWNSMAN.

                              As all men know
The virtues of your hundred-thousanders ;
They never hide their lights beneath a bushel.

STRANGER.

Nay, nay, uncharitable Sir ! for often
Doth bounty like a streamlet flow unseen,
Freshening and giving life along its course.

TOWNSMAN.

We track the streamlet by the brighter green
And livelier growth it gives ; .. but as for this ..
This was a pool that stagnated and stunk ;
The rains of heaven engendered nothing in it
But slime and foul corruption.

STRANGER.

                              Yet even these
Are reservoirs whence public charity
Still keeps her channels full.

TOWNSMAN.

                              Now, Sir, you touch
Upon the point.   This man of half a million

Had all these public virtues which you praise:
But the poor man rung never at his door,
And the old beggar, at the public gate,
Who, all the summer long, stands hat in hand,
He knew how vain it was to lift an eye
To that hard face.   Yet he was always found
Among your ten and twenty pound subscribers,
Your benefactors in the newspapers.
His alms were money put to interest
In the other world, .. donations to keep open
A running charity account with heaven, ..
Retaining fees against the Last Assizes,
When, for the trusted talents, strict account
Shall be required from all, and the old Arch-Lawyer
Plead his own cause as plaintiff.

STRANGER.

                   I must needs
Believe you, Sir : .. these are your witnesses,
These mourners here, who from their carriages
Gape at the gaping crowd.   A good March wind
Were to be pray'd for now, to lend their eyes
Some decent rheum; the very hireling mute
Bears not a face more blank of all emotion
Than the old servant of the family !
How can this man have lived, that thus his death
Costs not the soiling one white handkerchief!

TOWNSMAN.

Who should lament for him, Sir, in whose heart
Love had no place, nor natural charity ?

The parlour spaniel, when she heard his step,
Rose slowly from the hearth, and stole aside
With creeping pace ; she never raised her eyes
To woo kind words from him, nor laid her head
Upraised upon his knee, with fondling whine.
How could it be but thus ? Arithmetic
Was the sole science he was ever taught;
The multiplication-table was his Creed,
His Pater-noster, and his Decalogue.
When yet he was a boy, and should have breathed
The open air and sunshine of the fields,
To give his blood its natural spring and play,
He in a close and dusky counting-house
Smoke-dried and sear'd and shrivell'd up his heart.
So from the way in which he was train'd up
His feet departed not ; he toil'd and moil'd,
Poor muck-worm ! through his three-score years and
        ten ;
And when the earth shall now be shovell'd on him,
If that which served him for a soul were still
Within it's husk, 't would still be dirt to dirt.

                STRANGER.
Yet your next newspapers will blazon him
For industry and honourable wealth
A bright example.

                TOWNSMAN.
            Even half a million
Gets him no other praise.   But come this way

Some twelve months hence, and you will find his virtues
Trimly set forth in lapidary lines,
Faith with her torch beside, and little Cupids
Dropping upon his urn their marble tears.

Bristol, 1803.

NONDESCRIPTS.

I.

INSTALLATION AT OXFORD. 1793.

TOLL on, toll on, old Bell ! I 'll neither pass
The cold and weary hour in heartless rites,
Nor doze away the time.   The fire burns bright,
And, bless the maker of this Windsor-Chair !
(Of polish'd cherry, elbow'd, saddle-seated,)
This is the throne of comfort.   I will sit
And study here devoutly : .. not my Euclid, ..
For Heaven forbid that I should discompose
That Spider's excellent geometry !
I 'll study thee, Puss !   Not to make a picture,
I hate your canvass cats and dogs and fools,
Themes that disgrace the pencil.   Thou shalt give
A moral subject, Puss.   Come, look at me ; ..
Lift up thine emerald eyes !   Aye, purr away !
For I am praising thee, I tell thee, Puss,
And Cats as well as Kings like flattery.
For three whole days I heard an old Fur-gown
Bepraised, that made a Duke a Chancellor ;
Bepraised in prose it was, bepraised in verse ;
Lauded in pious Latin to the skies ;
Kudos'd egregiously in heathen Greek ;
In sapphics sweetly incensed ; glorified
In proud alcaics ; in hexameters

Applauded to the very Galleries
That did applaud again, whose thunder-claps,
Higher and longer with redoubling peals
Rung, when they heard the illustrious furbelow'd
Heroically in Popean rhyme
Tee-ti-tum'd, in Miltonic blank bemouth'd ;
Prose, verse, Greek, Latin, English, rhyme and blank,
Apotheosi-chancellor'd in all,
Till Eulogy, with all her wealth of words,
Grew bankrupt, all-too-prodigal of praise,
And panting Panegyric toil'd in vain
O'er-task'd in keeping pace with such desert.

　　Though I can poetize right willingly,
Puss, on thy well-streak'd coat, to that Fur-gown
I was not guilty of a single line :
'T was an old furbelow, that would hang loose,
And wrap round any one, as it were made
To fit him only, so it were but tied
With a blue ribband.
　　　　　　　　What a power there is
In beauty !   Within these forbidden walls
Thou hast thy range at will, and when perchance
The Fellows see thee, Puss, they overlook
Inhibitory laws, or haply think
The statute was not made for Cats like thee ;
For thou art beautiful as ever Cat
That wantoned in the joy of kittenhood.
Aye, stretch thy claws, thou democratic beast, ..
I like thine independence.   Treat thee well,
Thou art as playful as young Innocence ;
But if we act the governor, and break

The social compact, Nature gave those claws
And taught thee how to use them. Man, methinks,
Master and slave alike, might learn from thee
A salutary lesson: but the one
Abuses wickedly his power unjust,
The other crouches, spaniel-like, and licks
The hand that strikes him.   Wiser animal,
I look at thee, familiarised, yet free;
And, thinking that a child with gentle hand
Leads by a string the large-limb'd Elephant,
With mingled indignation and contempt
Behold his drivers goad the biped beast.

II.

SNUFF.

A DELICATE pinch! oh how it tingles up
The titillated nose, and fills the eyes
And breast, till in one comfortable sneeze
The full-collected pleasure bursts at last!
Most rare Columbus! thou shalt be for this
The only Christopher in my Kalendar.
Why but for thee the uses of the Nose
Were half unknown, and its capacity
Of joy.   The summer gale that from the heath,
At midnoon glowing with the golden gorse,
Bears its balsamic odour, but provokes
Not satisfies the sense; and all the flowers,
That with their unsubstantial fragrance tempt
And disappoint, bloom for so short a space,
That half the year the Nostrils would keep Lent,
But that the kind tobacconist admits
No winter in his work; when Nature sleeps
His wheels roll on, and still administer
A plenitude of joy, a tangible smell.

What are Peru and those Golcondan mines
To thee, Virginia? miserable realms,
The produce of inhuman toil, they send
Gold for the greedy, jewels for the vain.

But thine are *common* comforts ! .. To omit
Pipe-panegyric and tobacco-praise,
Think what the general joy the snuff-box gives,
Europe, and far above Pizarro's name
Write Raleigh in thy records of renown !
Him let the school-boy bless if he behold
His master's box produced, for when he sees
The thumb and finger of Authority
Stufft up the nostrils : when hat, head, and wig
Shake all ; when on the waistcoat black, brown dust,
From the oft reiterated pinch profuse
Profusely scattered, lodges in its folds,
And part on the magistral table lights,
Part on the open book, soon blown away,
Full surely soon shall then the brow severe
Relax ; and from vituperative lips
Words that of birch remind not, sounds of praise,
And jokes that *must* be laugh'd at shall proceed.

Westbury, 1799.

III.

COOL REFLECTIONS

DURING A MIDSUMMER WALK FROM WARMINSTER
TO SHAFTESBURY. 1799.

O SPARE me .. spare me, Phœbus ! if indeed
Thou hast not let another Phaëton
Drive earthward thy fierce steeds and fiery car;
Mercy ! I melt ! I melt ! No tree, no bush,
No shelter, not a breath of stirring air
East, West, or North, or South ! Dear God of day,
Put on thy nightcap; crop thy locks of light,
And be in the fashion; turn thy back upon us,
And let thy beams flow upward; make it night
Instead of noon; .. one little miracle,
In pity, gentle Phœbus !
                              What a joy,
Oh what a joy, to be a seal and flounder
On an ice island ! or to have a den
With the white bear, cavern'd in polar snow !
It were a comfort to shake hands with Death, ..
He has a rare cold hand ! to wrap one's self
In the gift shirt Dejanira sent,
Dipt in the blood of Nessus, just to keep
The sun off; or toast cheese for Beelzebub, ..
That were a cool employment to this journey

Along a road whose white intensity
Would now make platina uncongealable
Like quicksilver.
                Were it midnight, I should walk
Self-lanthorn'd, saturate with sunbeams. Jove!
O gentle Jove! have mercy, and once more
Kick that obdurate Phœbus out of heaven;
Give Boreas the wind-cholic, till he roar
For cardamum, and drink down peppermint,
Making what's left as precious as Tokay;
Send Mercury to salivate the sky
Till it dissolve in rain. O gentle Jove!
But some such little kindness to a wretch
Who feels his marrow spoiling his best coat,..
Who swells with calorique as if a Prester
Had leaven'd every limb with poison-yeast;..
Lend me thine eagle just to flap his wings
And fan me, and I will build temples to thee,
And turn true Pagan.
                Not a cloud nor breeze,..
O you most heathen Deities! if ever
My bones reach home (for, for the flesh upon them,
It hath resolved itself into a dew,)
I shall have learnt owl-wisdom. Thou vile Phœbus,
Set me a Persian sun-idolater
Upon this turnpike road, and I'll convert him
With no inquisitorial argument
But thy own fires. Now woe be to me, wretch,
That I was in a heretic country born!
Else might some mass for the poor souls that bleach,
And burn away the calx of their offences
In that great Purgatory crucible,

Help me. O Jupiter ! my poor complexion !
I am made a copper-Indian of already ;
And if no kindly cloud will parasol me,
My very cellular membrane will be changed, ..
I shall be negrofied.
                    A brook ! a brook !
O what a sweet cool sound !
                              'T is very nectar !
It runs like life through every strengthen'd limb !
Nymph of the stream, now take a grateful prayer.

  1799.

IV.

THE PIG.

A COLLOQUIAL POEM.

JACOB! I do not like to see thy nose
Turn'd up in scornful curve at yonder Pig.
It would be well, my friend, if we, like him,
Were perfect in our kind!.. And why despise
The sow-born grunter?.. He is obstinate,
Thou answerest; ugly, and the filthiest beast
That banquets upon offal.... Now I pray you
Hear the Pig's Counsel.

                Is he obstinate?
We must not, Jacob, be deceived by words;
We must not take them as unheeding hands
Receive base money at the current worth,
But with a just suspicion try their sound,
And in the even balance weigh them well.
See now to what this obstinacy comes:
A poor, mistreated, democratic beast,
He knows that his unmerciful drivers seek
Their profit, and not his. He hath not learnt
That Pigs were made for Man,.. born to be brawn'd
And baconized: that he must please to give
Just what his gracious masters please to take;
Perhaps his tusks, the weapons Nature gave
For self-defence, the general privilege;

Perhaps, .. hark Jacob ! dost thou hear that horn ?
Woe to the young posterity of Pork !
Their enemy is at hand.
                     Again. Thou say'st
The Pig is ugly. Jacob, look at him !
Those eyes have taught the Lover flattery.
His face, .. nay Jacob, Jacob ! were it fair
To judge a Lady in her dishabille ?
Fancy it drest, and with saltpetre rouged.
Behold his tail, my friend ; with curls like tha.
The wanton hop marries her stately spouse :
So crisp in beauty Amoretta's hair
Rings round her lover's soul the chains of love.
And what is beauty, but the aptitude
Of parts harmonious ? Give thy fancy scope,
And thou wilt find that no imagined change
Can beautify this beast.   Place at his end
The starry glories of the Peacock's pride,
Give him the Swan's white breast ; for his horn-hoofs
Shape such a foot and ankle as the waves
Crowded in eager rivalry to kiss
When Venus from the enamour'd sea arose ; ..
Jacob, thou canst but make a monster of him !
All alteration man could think, would mar
His Pig-perfection.
                 The last charge, .. he lives
A dirty life.   Here I could shelter him
With noble and right-reverend precedents,
And show by sanction of authority
That 't is a very honourable thing
To thrive by dirty ways.   But let me rest
On better ground the unanswerable defence.

The Pig is a philosopher, who knows
No prejudice.   Dirt ? . . Jacob, what is dirt ?
If matter, . . why the delicate dish that tempts
An o'ergorged Epicure to the last morsel
That stuffs him to the throat-gates, is no more.
If matter be not, but as Sages say,
Spirit is all, and all things visible
Are one, the infinitely modified,
Think, Jacob, what that Pig is, and the mire
Wherein he stands knee-deep !
                                   And there ! the breeze
Pleads with me, and has won thee to a smile
That speaks conviction.   O'er yon blossom'd field
Of beans it came, and thoughts of bacon rise.

Westbury, 1799.

V.

THE DANCING BEAR.

RECOMMENDED TO THE ADVOCATES FOR THE
SLAVE-TRADE.

RARE music! I would rather hear cat-courtship
Under my bed-room window in the night,
Than this scraped catgut's screak. Rare dancing too!
Alas, poor Bruin! How he foots the pole
And waddles round it with unwieldly steps,
Swaying from side to side !.. The dancing-master
Hath had as profitless a pupil in him
As when he would have tortured my poor toes
To minuet grace, and made them move like clockwork
In musical obedience. Bruin! Bruin!
Thou art but a clumsy biped !.. And the mob
With noisy merriment mock his heavy pace,
And laugh to see him led by the nose !.. themselves
Led by the nose, embruted, and in the eye
Of Reason from their Nature's purposes
As miserably perverted.
                                Bruin-Bear !
Now could I sonnetize thy piteous plight,
And prove how much my sympathetic heart
Even for the miseries of a beast can feel,
In fourteen lines of sensibility.

But we are told all things were made for Man;
And I'll be sworn there's not a fellow here
Who would not swear 'twere hanging blasphemy
To doubt that truth.   Therefore as thou wert born,
Bruin! for Man, and Man makes nothing of thee
In any other way, ... most logically
It follows, thou wert born to make him sport;
That that great snout of thine was form'd on purpose
To hold a ring; and that thy fat was given thee
For an approved pomatum!
      To demur
Were heresy.   And politicians say,
(Wise men who in the scale of reason give
No foolish feelings weight,) that thou art here
Far happier than thy brother Bears who roam
O'er trackless snow for food; that being born
Inferior to thy leader, unto him
Rightly belongs dominion; that the compact
Was made between ye, when thy clumsy feet
First fell into the snare, and he gave up
His right to kill, conditioning thy life
Should thenceforth be his property; .. besides,
'T is wholesome for thy morals to be brought
From savage climes into a civilized state,
Into the decencies of Christendom.....
Bear! Bear! it passes in the Parliament
For excellent logic this! What if we say
How barbarously Man abuses power?
Talk of thy baiting, it will be replied,
Thy welfare is thy owner's interest,
But were thou baited it would injure thee,

Therefore thou art not baited.   For seven years
Hear it, O Heaven, and give ear, O Earth !
For seven long years this precious syllogism
Hath baffled justice and humanity !

Westbury, 1799.

VI.

THE FILBERT.

NAY, gather not that Filbert, Nicholas,
There is a maggot there, .. it is his house, ..
His castle, .. oh commit not burglary !
Strip him not naked, .. 't is his clothes, his shell,
His bones, the case and armour of his life,
And thou shalt do no murder, Nicholas !
It were an easy thing to crack that nut
Or with thy crackers or thy double teeth,
So easily may all things be destroy'd !
But 't is not in the power of mortal man
To mend the fracture of a filbert shell.
There were two great men once amused themselves
Watching two maggots run their wriggling race,
And wagering on their speed ; but Nick, to us
It were no sport to see the pamper'd worm
Roll out and then draw in his folds of fat,
Like to some Barber's leathern powder-bag
Wherewith he feathers, frosts, or cauliflowers
Spruce Beau, or Lady fair, or Doctor grave.
Enough of dangers and of enemies
Hath Nature's wisdom for the worm ordain'd,
Increase not thou the number !   Him the Mouse
Gnawing with nibbling tooth the shell's defence,
May from his native tenement eject ;

Him may the Nut-hatch, piercing with strong bill,
Unwittingly destroy ; or to his hoard
The Squirrel bear, at leisure to be crack'd.
Man also hath his dangers and his foes
As this poor Maggot hath; and when I muse
Upon the aches, anxieties, and fears,
The Maggot knows not, Nicholas, methinks
It were a happy metamorphosis
To be enkernell'd thus : never to hear
Of wars, and of invasions, and of plots,
Kings, Jacobines, and Tax-commissioners ;
To feel no motion but the wind that shook
The Filbert Tree, and rock'd us to our rest ;
And in the middle of such exquisite food
To live luxurious !   The perfection this
Of snugness ! it were to unite at once
Hermit retirement, Aldermanic bliss,
And Stoic independence of mankind.

Westbury, 1799.

VII.

THE CATARACT OF LODORE.

DESCRIBED IN RHYMES FOR THE NURSERY.

" How does the Water,
Come down at Lodore ? "
My little boy ask'd me
Thus, once on a time ;
And moreover he task'd me
To tell him in rhyme.
Anon at the word,
There first came one daughter
And then came another,
To second and third
The request of their brother,
And to hear how the Water
Comes down at Lodore,
With its rush and its roar.
As many a time
They had seen it before.
So I told them in rhyme,
For of rhymes I had store ;
And 't was in my vocation
For their recreation
That so I should sing ;
Because I was Laureate
To them and the King.

From its sources which well
In the Tarn on the fell;
From its fountains
In the mountains,
It's rills and it's gills;
Through moss and through brake,
It runs and it creeps
For awhile, till it sleeps
In its own little Lake.
And thence at departing,
Awakening and starting,
It runs through the reeds
᾽And away it proceeds,
Through meadow and glade,
In sun and in shade,
And through the wood-shelter,
Among crags in its flurry,
Helter-skelter,
Hurry-scurry.
Here it comes sparkling,
And there it lies darkling;
Now smoaking and frothing
It's tumult and wrath in,
Till in this rapid race
On which it is bent,
It reaches the place
Of its steep descent.

The Cataract strong
Then plunges along,
Striking and raging
As if a war waging
Its caverns and rocks among:

Rising and leaping,
Sinking and creeping,
Swelling and sweeping,
Showering and springing,
Flying and flinging,
Writhing and ringing,
Eddying and whisking,
Spouting and frisking,
Turning and twisting,
Around and around
With endless rebound ;
Smiting and fighting,
A sight to delight in ;
Confounding, astounding,
Dizzying and deafening the ear with its sound.

Collecting, projecting,
Receding and speeding,
And shocking and rocking,
And darting and parting,
And threading and spreading,
And whizzing and hissing,
And dripping and skipping,
And hitting and splitting,
And shining and twining,
And rattling and battling,
And shaking and quaking,
And pouring and roaring,
And waving and raving,
And tossing and crossing,
And flowing and going,
And running and stunning,

And foaming and roaming,
And dinning and spinning,
And dropping and hopping,
And working and jerking,
And guggling and struggling,
And heaving and cleaving,
And moaning and groaning ;

And glittering and frittering,
And gathering and feathering,
And whitening and brightening,
And quivering and shivering,
And hurrying and skurrying,
And thundering and floundering;

Dividing and gliding and sliding,
And falling and brawling and sprawling,
And driving and riving and striving,
And sprinkling and twinkling and wrinkling,
And sounding and bounding and rounding,
And bubbling and troubling and doubling,
And grumbling and rumbling and tumbling,
And clattering and battering and shattering ;

Retreating and beating and meeting and sheeting,
Delaying and straying and playing and spraying,
Advancing and prancing and glancing and dancing,
Recoiling, turmoiling and toiling and boiling,
And gleaming and streaming and steaming and
         beaming,
And rushing and flushing and brushing and gushing,
And flapping and rapping and clapping and slapping,

And curling and whirling and purling and twirling,
And thumping and plumping and bumping and
    jumping,
And dashing and flashing and splashing and clashing;
And so never ending, but always descending,
Sounds and motions for ever and ever are blending,
All at once and all o'er, with a mighty uproar,
And this way the Water comes down at Lodore.

Keswick, 1820.

VIII.

ROBERT THE RHYMER'S
TRUE AND PARTICULAR ACCOUNT OF HIMSELF.

ROBERT the Rhymer who lives at the Lakes
Describes himself thus, to prevent mistakes ;
Or rather, perhaps, be it said, to correct them,
There being plenty about for those who collect them.
He is lean of body, and lank of limb ;
The man must walk fast who would overtake him.
His eyes are not yet much the worse for the wear,
And Time has not thinn'd nor straighten'd his hair,
Notwithstanding that now he is more than halfway
On the road from Grizzle to Gray.
He hath a long nose with a bending ridge ;
It might be worthy of notice on Strasburg bridge.
He sings like a lark when at morn he arises,
And when evening comes he nightingalizes,
Warbling house-notes wild from throat and gizzard,
Which reach from A to G, and from G to Izzard.
His voice is as good as when he was young,
And he has teeth enough left to keep-in his tongue.
A man he is by nature merry,
Somewhat Tom-foolish, and comical, very ;
Who has gone through the world, not mindful of pelf,
Upon easy terms, thank Heaven, with himself,
Along bypaths and in pleasant ways,
Caring as little for censure as praise ;

Having some friends whom he loves dearly,
And no lack of foes, whom he laughs at sincerely ;
And never for great, nor for little things,
Has he fretted his guts to fiddle-strings.
He might have made them by such folly
Most musical, most melancholy.

Sic cecinit Robertus, anno ætatis suæ *55.*

THE DEVIL'S WALK.

ADVERTISEMENT.

AFTER the Devil's Thoughts had been published by Mr. Coleridge in the collection of his Poetical Works, and the statement with which he accompanied it, it might have been supposed that the joint authorship of that Siamese production had been sufficiently authenticated, and that no supposititious claim to it would again be advanced. The following extract, however, appeared in the *John Bull* of Feb. 14. 1830 : —

" In the *Morning Post* of Tuesday, we find the following letter : —

" ' *To the Editor of the Morning Post.*

" ' SIR,—Permit me to correct a statement which appeared in a recent number of the *John Bull,* wherein it is made to appear that Dr. Southey is the author of the Poem entitled *The Devil's Walk.* I have the means of settling this question ; since I possess the identical MS. copy of verses, as they

G 2

were written by my uncle, the late Professor Porson,
during an evening party at Dr. Beloe's.

        " ' I am Sir, your very obedient servant,

                     " ' R. C. PORSON.

" ' *Bayswater Terrace*, Feb. 6. 1830.'

    " We are quite sure that Mr. Porson, the writer
of the above letter, is convinced of the truth of the
statement it contains ; but although *The Devil's
Walk* is perhaps not a work of which either
Mr. Southey or Mr. Porson need be very proud,
we feel it due to ourselves to re-state the fact of its
being from the pen of Mr. Southey. If we are
wrong, Mr. Porson may apply to Mr. Southey; for
although Mr. Porson's eminent uncle is dead, the
Poet Laureate is alive and merry.

    "The Lines—Poem they can scarcely be called—
were written by Mr. Southey, one morning before
breakfast, the idea having struck him while he was
shaving ; they were subsequently shown to Mr.
Coleridge, who, we believe, pointed some of the
stanzas, and perhaps added one or two.

    " We beg to assure Mr. R. C. Porson that we recur
to this matter out of no disrespect either to the
memory of his uncle, which is not likely to be
affected one way or another, by the circumstance ;
or to his own veracity, being, as we said, quite assured that he believes the statement he makes : our
only object is to set ourselves right."

* * * * *

" Our readers, perhaps, may smile at the following, which appears in yesterday's *Court Journal:* —

" ' We have received a letter, signed " W. Marshall," and dated "York;" claiming for its writer the long-contested authorship of those celebrated verses, which are known by the title of *The Devil's Walk on Earth,* and to which attention has lately been directed anew, by Lord Byron's imitation of them. There have been so many mystifications connected with the authorship of these clever verses, that, for any thing we know to the contrary, this letter may be only one more.' "

* * * * *

A week afterwards there was the following notice: —" We cannot waste any more time about *The Devil's Walk.* We happen to *know* that it is Mr. Southey's ; but, as he is alive, we refer any body, who is not yet satisfied, to the eminent person himself—we do not mean the Devil—but the Doctor."

The same newspaper contained the ensuing advertisement : — " On Tuesday next, uniform with Robert Cruikshank's Monsieur Tonson, price one shilling : The Devil's Walk, a Poem, by Professor Porson. With additions and variations by Southey and Coleridge; illustrated by seven engravings from R. Cruikshank. London, Marsh and Miller,

137. Oxford Street; and Constable and Co., Edinburgh."

Professor Porson never had any part in these
verses as a *writer,* and it is for the first time that
he now appears in them as the *subject* of two or
three stanzas written some few years ago, when
the fabricated story of his having composed them
during an evening party at Dr. Vincent's (for that
was the original *habitat* of this falsehood) was re-
vived. A friend of one of the authors, more jealous
for him than he has ever been for himself, urged
him then to put the matter out of doubt (for it was
before Mr. Coleridge had done so); and as much
to please that friend, as to amuse himself and his
domestic circle, in a sportive mood, the part which
relates the rise and progress of the Poem was thrown
off, and that also touching the aforesaid Professor.
The old vein having thus been opened, some other
passages were added ; and so it grew to its present
length.

THE DEVIL'S WALK.

1.

Fʀᴏᴍ his brimstone bed at break of day
   A walking the Devil is gone,
To look at his little snug farm of the World
   And see how his stock went on.

2.

Over the hill and over the dale,
   And he went over the plain;
And backward and forward he swish'd his tail,
   As a gentleman swishes a cane.

3.

   How then was the Devil drest?
   Oh, he was in his Sunday's best
His coat was red and his breeches were blue,
And there was a hole where his tail came through

4.

A lady drove by in her pride,
In whose face an expression he spied

For which he could have kiss'd her ;
Such a flourishing, fine, clever creature was she,
With an eye as wicked as wicked can be,
I should take her for my Aunt, thought he,
   If my dam had had a sister.

5.

   He met a lord of high degree,
   No matter what was his name ;
Whose face with his own when he came to compare
   The expression, the look, and the air,
   And the character too, as it seem'd to a hair, —
Such a twin-likeness there was in the pair
That it made the Devil start and stare,
For he thought there was surely a looking-glass there,
   But he could not see the frame.

6.

He saw a Lawyer killing a viper
   On a dunghill beside his stable ;
Ho! quoth he, thou put'st me in mind
   Of the story of Cain and Abel.

7.

An Apothecary on a white horse
   Rode by on his vocation ;
And the Devil thought of his old friend
   Death in the Revelation.

8.

He pass'd a cottage with a double coach-house,
   A cottage of gentility.

And he own'd with a grin
That his favourite sin
  Is pride that apes humility.

9.

He saw a pig rapidly
  Down a river float;
The pig swam well, but every stroke
  Was cutting his own throat;

10.

And Satan gave thereat his tail
  A twirl of admiration;
For he thought of his daughter War
  And her suckling babe Taxation.

11.

Well enough, in sooth, he liked that truth,
  And nothing the worse for the jest;
But this was only a first thought
  And in this he did not rest:
Another came presently into his head
And here it proved, as has often been said,
  That second thoughts are best.

12

For as Piggy plied with wind and tide,
  His way with such celerity,
And at every stroke the water dyed
With his own red blood, the Devil cried,
Behold a swinish nation's pride
  In cotton-spun prosperity.

13.

He walk'd into London leisurely,
  The streets were dirty and dim:
But there he saw Brothers the Prophet,
  And Brothers the Prophet saw him.*

14.

He entered a thriving bookseller's shop;
  Quoth he, We are both of one college,
For I myself sate like a Cormorant once
  Upon the Tree of Knowledge.

15.

As he passed through Cold-Bath Fields he look'd
  At a solitary cell;
And he was well-pleased, for it gave him a hint
  For improving the prisons of Hell.

16.

He saw a turnkey tie a thief's hands
  With a cordial tug and jerk;
Nimbly, quoth he, a man's fingers move
  When his heart is in his work.

17.

He saw the same turnkey unfettering a man
  With little expedition;
And he chuckled to think of his dear slave trade,
And the long debates and delays that were made
  Concerning its abolition.

* " After this I was in a vision, having the angel of God
near me, and saw Satan walking leisurely into London." —
Brothers' Prophecies, part i. p. 41.

18.

He met one of his favourite daughters
    By an Evangelical Meeting ;
And forgetting himself for joy at her sight,
He would have accosted her outright,.
    And given her a fatherly greeting.

19.

But she tipt him a wink, drew back, and cried,
    Avaunt ! my name 's Religion !
And then she turn'd to the preacher
    And leer'd like a love-sick pigeon.

20.

A fine man and a famous Professor was he,
As the great Alexander now may be,
    Whose fame not yet o'erpast is ;
Or that new Scotch performer
Who is fiercer and warmer,
    The great Sir Arch-Bombastes.

21.

With throbs and throes, and ahs and ohs,
    Far famed his flock for frightening ;
And thundering with his voice, the while
    His eyes zigzag like lightning.

22.

This Scotch phenomenon, I trow,
    Beats Alexander hollow ;

Even when most tame
He breathes more flame
   Than ten Fire-Kings could swallow.

23.

Another daughter he presently met:
   With music of fife and drum,
   And a consecrated flag,
   And shout of tag and rag,
   And march of rank and file,
Which had fill'd the crowded aisle
   Of the venerable pile,
From church he saw her come.

24.

He call'd her aside, and began to chide,
   For what dost thou here ? said he :
   My city of Rome is thy proper home,
   And there 's work enough there for thee

25.

   Thou hast confessions to listen,
   And bells to christen,
And altars and dolls to dress ;
   And fools to coax,
   And sinners to hoax,
And beads and bones to bless ;
   And great pardons to sell
   For those who pay well,
And small ones for those who pay less.

26.

Nay, Father, I boast, that this is my post,
  She answered; and thou wilt allow,
    That the great Harlot,
    Who is clothed in scarlet,
  Can very well spare me now.

27.

Upon her business I am come here,
    That we may extend her powers;
Whatever lets down this church that we hate,
    Is something in favour of ours.

28.

You will not think, great Cosmocrat!
    That I spend my time in fooling;
Many irons, my Sire, have we in the fire,
    And I must leave none of them cooling;
For you must know state-councils here
    Are held which I bear rule in.
      When my liberal notions
      Produce mischievous motions,
      There 's many a man of good intent,
    In either house of Parliament,
      Whom I shall find a tool in;
    And I have hopeful pupils too
      Who all this while are schooling.

29.

Fine progress they make in our liberal opinions,
    My Utilitarians.,

My all sorts of — inians
    And all sorts of — arians ;
    My all sorts of — ists,
And my Prigs and my Whigs
    Who have all sorts of twists
Train'd in the very way, I know,
Father, you would have them go ;
        High and low,
    Wise and foolish, great and small,
    March-of-Intellect-Boys all.

30.

Well pleased wilt thou be at no very far day
    When the   caldron of mischief boils,
    And I bring them forth in battle array
    And bid them suspend their broils,
    That they may unite and fall on the prey,
        For which we are spreading our toils.
How the nice boys all will give mouth at the call,
        Hark away ! hark away to the spoils!
My Macs and my Quacks and my lawless-Jacks,
My Shiels and O'Connells, my pious Mac-Donnells,
    My joke-smith Sidney, and all of his kidney,
        My Humes and my Broughams,
            My merry old Jerry,
    My Lord Kings, and my Doctor Doyles !

31.

At this good news, so great
    The Devil's pleasure grew,
That with a joyful swish he rent
    The hole where his tail came through,

32.

His countenance fell for a moment
  When he felt the stitches go
Ah! thought he, there's a job now
  That I've made for my tailor below.

33

Great news! bloody news! cried a newsman ;
  The Devil said, Stop, let me see !
Great news? bloody news? thought the Devil,
  The bloodier the better for me.

34.

So he bought the newspaper, and no news
  At all, for his money he had.
Lying varlet, thought he, thus to take in old Nick !
  But it's some satisfaction, my lad,
To know thou art paid beforehand for the trick,
  For the sixpence I gave thee is bad.

35.

And then it came into his head
  By oracular inspiration,
That what he had seen and what he had said,
  In the course of this visitation,
Would be published in the Morning Post
  For all this reading nation.

36.

Therewith in second-sight he saw
  The place and the manner and time,
In which this mortal story
  Would be put in immortal rhyme.

37.

That it would happen when two poets
  Should on a time be met,
In the town of Nether Stowey,
  In the shire of Somerset.

38.

There while the one was shaving
  Would he the song begin ;
And the other when he heard it at breakfast,
  In ready accord join in.

39.

So each would help the other,
  Two heads being better than one ;
    And the phrase and conceit
    Would in unison meet,
And so with glee the verse flow free,
  In ding-dong chime of sing-song rhyme,
    Till the whole were merrily done.

40.

And because it was set to the razor,
  Not to the lute or harp,
Therefore it was that the fancy
Should be bright, and the wit be sharp.

41.

But then, said Satan to himself,
  As for that said beginner,
Against my infernal Majesty
  There is no greater sinner.

42.

He hath put me in ugly ballads
  With libellous pictures for sale ;
He hath scoff'd at my hoofs and my horns,
  And has made very free with my tail.

43.

But this Mister Poet shall find
  I am not a safe subject for whim ;
For I'll set up a School of my own,
  And my Poets shall set upon him.

44.

He went to a coffee-house to dine,
  And there he had soy in his dish ;
Having ordered some soles for his dinner,
  Because he was fond of flat fish.

45.

They are much to my palate, thought he,
  And now guess the reason who can,
Why no bait should be better than place,
  When I fish for a Parliament-man.

46.

But the soles in the bill were ten shillings;
  Tell your master, quoth he, what I say ;
If he charges at this rate for all things,
  He must be in a pretty good way.

47.

But mark ye, said he to the waiter,
　I 'm a dealer myself in this line,
And his business, between you and me,
　Nothing like so extensive as mine.

48.

Now soles are exceedingly cheap ;
　Which he will not attempt to deny,
When I see him at my fish-market,
　I warrant him, by and by.

49.

As he went along the Strand
　Between three in the morning and four,
He observed a queer-looking person
　Who stagger'd from Perry's door.

50.

And he thought that all the world over
　In vain for a man you might seek,
Who could drink more like a Trojan
　Or talk more like a Greek.

51.

The Devil then he prophesied
It would one day be matter of talk,
　That with wine when smitten,
And with wit moreover being happily bitten,
This erudite bibber was he who had written
　The story of this walk.

52.

A pretty mistake, quoth the Devil;
    A pretty mistake I opine !
I have put many ill thoughts in his mouth,
    He will never put good ones in mine.

53.

And whoever shall say that to Porson
    These best of all verses belong,
He is an untruth-telling whoreson,
    And so shall be call'd in the song.

54.

And if seeking an illicit connection with fame,
    Any one else should put in a claim,
        In this comical competition ;
    That excellent poem will prove
        A man-trap for such foolish ambition,
Where the silly rogue shall be caught by the leg,
    And exposed in a second edition.

55.

Now the morning air was cold for him
    Who was used to a warm abode ;
And yet he did not immediately wish,
    To set out on his homeward road.

56.

For he had some morning calls to make
    Before he went back to Hell;

H 2

So thought he I 'll step into a gaming-house,
  And that will do as well;
But just before he could get to the door
  A wonderful chance befell.

57.

For all on a sudden, in a dark place,
He came upon General ————'s burning face ;
  And it struck him with such consternation,
That home in a hurry his way did he take,
Because he thought by a slight mistake
  'T was the general conflagration.

INSCRIPTIONS.

THE three utilities of Poetry: the praise of Virtue and Goodness, the memory of things remarkable, and to invigorate the Affections.

Welsh Triad.

I.

CALLEST thou thyself a Patriot? .. On this field
Did Falkland fall, the blameless and the brave,
Beneath the banners of that Charles whom thou
Abhorrest for a Tyrant.   Dost thou boast
Of loyalty?   The field is not far off
Where in rebellious arms against his King
Hambden was kill'd, that Hambden at whose name
The heart of many an honest Englishman
Beats with congenial pride.   Both uncorrupt,
Friends to their common country both, they fought,
They died in adverse armies.   Traveller!
If with thy neighbour thou shouldst not accord,
Remember these, our famous countrymen,
And quell all angry and injurious thoughts.

Bristol, 1796.

II.

FOR A CAVERN THAT OVERLOOKS THE RIVER AVON.

ENTER this cavern, Stranger! Here awhile
Respiring from the long and steep ascent,
Thou may'st be glad of rest, and haply too
Of shade, if from the summer's westering sun
Shelter'd beneath this beetling vault of rock.
Round the rude portal clasping its rough arms
The antique ivy spreads a canopy,
From whose grey blossoms the wild bees collect
In autumn their last store. The Muses love
This spot; believe a Poet who hath felt
Their visitation here. The tide below
Rising or refluent scarcely sends its sound
Of waters up ; and from the heights beyond
Where the high-hanging forest waves and sways,
Varying before the wind its verdant hues,
The voice is music here. Here thou may'st feel
How good, how lovely, Nature! And when hence
Returning to the city's crowded streets,
Thy sickening eye at every step revolts
From scenes of vice and wretchedness, reflect
That Man creates the evil he endures.

Bristol, 1796.

III.

FOR A TABLET AT SILBURY-HILL.

THIS mound in some remote and dateless day
Rear'd o'er a Chieftain of the Age of Hills,
May here detain thee, Traveller ! from thy road
Not idly lingering.   In his narrow house
Some Warrior sleeps below, whose gallant deeds
Haply at many a solemn festival
The Scald hath sung ; but perish'd is the song
Of praise, as o'er these bleak and barren downs
The wind that passes and is heard no more.
Go, Traveller, and remember when the pomp
Of earthly Glory fades, that one good deed,
Unseen, unheard, unnoted by mankind,
Lives in the eternal register of Heaven.

Bristol, 1796.

IV.

FOR A MONUMENT IN THE NEW FOREST.

THIS is the place where William's kingly power
Did from their poor and peaceful homes expel,
Unfriended, desolate, and shelterless,
The habitants of all the fertile track
Far as these wilds extend.   He levell'd down
Their little cottages, he bade their fields
Lie waste, and forested the land, that so
More royally might he pursue his sports.
If that thine heart be human, Passenger !
Sure it will swell within thee, and thy lips
Will mutter curses on him.   Think thou then
What cities flame, what hosts unsepulchred
Pollute the passing wind, when raging Power
Drives on his blood-hounds to the chase of Man ;
And as thy thoughts anticipate that day
When God shall judge aright, in charity
Pray for the wicked rulers of mankind.

Bristol, 1796.

V.

FOR A TABLET ON THE BANKS OF A STREAM.

STRANGER ! awhile upon this mossy bank
Recline thee. If the Sun rides high, the breeze,
That loves to ripple o'er the rivulet,
Will play around thy brow, and the cool sound
Of running waters soothe thee. Mark how clear
They sparkle o'er the shallows, and behold
Where o'er their surface wheels with restless speed
Yon glossy insect, on the sand below
How its swift shadow flits. In solitude
The rivulet is pure, and trees and herbs,
Bend o'er its salutary course refresh'd,
But passing on amid the haunts of men,
It finds pollution there, and rolls from thence
A tainted stream. Seek'st thou for HAPPINESS ?
Go, Stranger, sojourn in the woodland cot
Of INNOCENCE, and thou shalt find her there.

Bristol, 1796.

VI.

FOR THE CENOTAPH AT ERMENONVILLE.

STRANGER! the MAN of NATURE lies not here:
Enshrined far distant by the Scoffer's * side
His relics rest, there by the giddy throng
With blind idolatry alike revered.
Wiselier directed have thy pilgrim feet
Explored the scenes of Ermenonville. ROUSSEAU
Loved these calm haunts of Solitude and Peace;
Here he has heard the murmurs of the lake,
And the soft rustling of the poplar grove,
When o'er its bending boughs the passing wind
Swept a gray shade. Here, if thy breast be full,
If in thine eye the tear devout should gush,
His SPIRIT shall behold thee, to thine home
From hence returning, purified of heart.

Bristol, 1796.

* Voltaire.

VII.

FOR A MONUMENT AT OXFORD.

HERE Latimer and Ridley in the flames
Bore witness to the truth. If thou hast walk'd
Uprightly through the world, just thoughts of joy
May fill thy breast in contemplating here
Congenial virtue. But if thou hast swerved
From the straight path of even rectitude,
Fearful in trying seasons to assert
The better cause, or to forsake the worse
Reluctant, when perchance therein enthrall'd
Slave to false shame, oh ! thankfully receive
The sharp compunctious motions that this spot
May wake within thee, and be wise in time,
And let the future for the past atone.

Bath, 1797.

VIII.

FOR A MONUMENT IN THE VALE OF EWIAS.

HERE was it, Stranger, that the patron Saint
Of Cambria pass'd his age of penitence,
A solitary man ; and here he made
His hermitage, the roots his food, his drink
Of Hodney's mountain stream. Perchance thy youth
Has read with eager wonder how the Knight
Of Wales in Ormandine's enchanted bower
Slept the long sleep : and if that in thy veins
Flow the pure blood of Britain, sure that blood
Hath flow'd with quicker impulse at the tale
Of David's deeds, when through the press of war
His gallant comrades follow'd his green crest
To victory. Stranger! Hatterill's mountain heights
And this fair vale of Ewias, and the stream
Of Hodney, to thine after-thoughts will rise
More grateful, thus associate with the name
Of David and the deeds of other days.

Bath, 1798.

IX.

EPITAPH ON ALGERNON SYDNEY.

HERE Sidney lies, he whom perverted law,
The pliant jury and the bloody judge,
Doom'd to a traitor's death.   A tyrant King
Required, an abject country saw and shared
The crime.   The noble cause of Liberty
He loved in life, and to that noble cause
In death bore witness.   But his Country rose
Like Samson from her sleep, and broke her chains,
And proudly with her worthies she enroll'd
Her murder'd Sidney's name.   The voice of man
Gives honour or destroys ; but earthly power
Gives not, nor takes away, the self-applause
Which on the scaffold suffering virtue feels,
Nor that which God appointed its reward.

Westbury, 1798.

X.

EPITAPH ON KING JOHN.

JOHN rests below.   A man more infamous
Never hath held the sceptre of these realms,
And bruised beneath the iron rod of Power
The oppressed men of England.   Englishman !
Curse not his memory.   Murderer as he was,
Coward and slave, yet he it was who sign'd
That Charter which should make thee morn and night
Be thankful for thy birth-place : ... Englishman !
That holy Charter, which, shouldst thou permit
Force to destroy, or Fraud to undermine,
Thy children's groans will persecute thy soul,
For they must bear the burthen of thy crime.

Westbury, 1798.

XI.

IN A FOREST.

STRANGER! whose steps have reach'd this solitude,
Know that this lonely spot was dear to one
Devoted with no unrequited zeal
To Nature. Here, delighted he has heard
The rustling of these woods, that now perchance
Melodious to the gale of summer move;
And underneath their shade on yon smooth rock,
With grey and yellow lichens overgrown,
Often reclined; watching the silent flow
Of this perspicuous rivulet, that steals
Along its verdant course, .. till all around
Had fill'd his senses with tranquillity,
And ever soothed in spirit he return'd
A happier, better man. Stranger! perchance,
Therefore the stream more lovely to thine eye
Will glide along, and to the summer gale
The woods wave more melodious. Cleanse thou then
The weeds and mosses from this letter'd stone.

Westbury, 1798.

XII.

FOR A MONUMENT AT TORDESILLAS.

SPANIARD ! if thou art one who bows the knee
Before a despot's footstool, hie thee hence !
This ground is holy : here Padilla died,
Martyr of Freedom.   But if thou dost love
Her cause, stand then as at an altar here,
And thank the Almighty that thine honest heart,
Full of a brother's feelings for mankind,
Revolts against oppression.   Not unheard
Nor unavailing shall the grateful prayer
Ascend ; for honest impulses will rise,
Such as may elevate and strengthen thee
For virtuous action.   Relics silver-shrined,
And chaunted mass, would wake within the soul
Thoughts valueless and cold compared with these.

Bristol, 1796.

XIII.

FOR A COLUMN AT TRUXILLO.

PIZARRO here was born; a greater name
The list of Glory boasts not. Toil and Pain,
Famine and hostile Elements, and Hosts
Embattled, fail'd to check him in his course,
Not to be wearied, not to be deterr'd,
Not to be overcome. A mighty realm
He over-ran, and with relentless arm
Slew or enslaved its unoffending sons,
And wealth, and power, and fame, were his rewards.
There is another world, beyond the Grave,
According to their deeds where men are judged.
O Reader! if thy daily bread be earn'd
By daily labour, .. yea, however low,
However painful be thy lot assign'd,
Thank thou, with deepest gratitude, the God
Who made thee, that thou art not such as he.

Bristol, 1796.

XIV.

FOR THE CELL OF HONORIUS, AT THE CORK CONVENT, NEAR CINTRA.

HERE cavern'd like a beast Honorius pass d
In self-affliction, solitude, and prayer,
Long years of penance.   He had rooted out
All human feelings from his heart, and fled
With fear and loathing from all human joys.
Not thus in making known his will divine
Hath Christ enjoin'd.   To aid the fatherless,
Comfort the sick, and be the poor man's friend,
And in the wounded heart pour gospel-balm;
These are the injunctions of his holy law,
Which whoso keeps shall have a joy on earth,
Calm, constant, still increasing, preluding
The eternal bliss of Heaven.   Yet mock not thou,
Stranger, the Anchorite's mistaken zeal !
He painfully his painful duties kept,
Sincere though erring : Stranger, do thou keep
Thy better and thine easier rule as well.

Bristol, 1798.

XV.

FOR A MONUMENT AT TAUNTON.

THEY suffer'd here whom Jefferies doom'd to death
In mockery of all justice, when the Judge
Unjust, subservient to a cruel King,
Perform'd his work of blood.   They suffer'd here
The victims of that Judge, and of that King;
In mockery of all justice here they bled,
Unheard.   But not unpitied, nor of God
Unseen, the innocent suffered; not unheard
The innocent blood cried vengeance; for at length
The indignant Nation in its power arose,
Resistless.   Then that wicked Judge took flight,
Disguised in vain:.. not always is the Lord
Slow to revenge!   A miserable man
He fell beneath the people's rage, and still
The children curse his memory.   From the throne
The obdurate bigot who commission'd him,
Inhuman James, was driven.   He lived to drag
Long years of frustrate hope, he lived to load
More blood upon his soul.   Let tell the Boyne,
Let Londonderry tell his guilt and shame;
And that immortal day when on thy shores,
La Hogue, the purple ocean dash'd the dead!

Westbury, 1798.

I 3

XVI.

FOR A TABLET AT PENSHURST.

ARE days of old familiar to thy mind,
O Reader?   Hast thou let the midnight hour
Pass unperceived, whilst thou in fancy lived
With high-born beauties and enamour'd chiefs,
Sharing their hopes, and with a breathless joy
Whose expectation touch'd the verge of pain,
Following their dangerous fortunes? If such lore
Hath ever thrill'd thy bosom, thou wilt tread,
As with a pilgrim's reverential thoughts,
The groves of Penshurst.   Sydney here was born,
Sydney, than whom no gentler, braver man
His own delightful genius ever feign'd,
Illustrating the vales of Arcady
With courteous courage and with loyal loves.
Upon his natal day an acorn here
Was planted : it grew up a stately oak,
And in the beauty of its strength it stood
And flourish'd, when his perishable part
Had moulder'd, dust to dust.   That stately oak
Itself hath moulder'd now, but Sydney's fame
Endureth in his own immortal works.

Westbury, 1799.

XVII.

EPITAPH.

THIS to a mother's sacred memory
Her son hath hallow'd.   Absent many a year
Far over sea, his sweetest dreams were still
Of that dear voice which soothed his infancy ;
And after many a fight against the Moor
And Malabar, or that fierce cavalry
Which he had seen covering the boundless plain,
Even to the utmost limits where the eye
Could pierce the far horizon, .. his first thought
In safety was of her, who when she heard
The tale of that day's danger, would retire
And pour her pious gratitude to Heaven
In prayers and tears of joy.   The lingering hour
Of his return, long-look'd-for, came at length,
And full of hope he reach'd his native shore.
Vain hope that puts its trust in human life !
For ere he came, the number of her days
Was full.   O Reader, what a world were this,
How unendurable its weight, if they
Whom Death hath sunder'd did not meet again !

Keswick, 1810.

I 4

XVIII.

EPITAPH.

HERE in the fruitful vales of Somerset
Was Emma born, and here the Maiden grew
To the sweet season of her womanhood
Beloved and lovely, like a plant whose leaf
And bud and blossom all are beautiful.
In peacefulness her virgin years were past;
And when in prosperous wedlock she was given,
Amid the Cumbrian mountains far away
She had her summer Bower. 'T was like a dream
Of old Romance to see her when she plied
Her little skiff on Derwent's glassy lake;
The roseate evening resting on the hills,
The lake returning back the hues of heaven,
Mountains and vales and waters all imbued
With beauty, and in quietness; and she,
Nymph-like, amid that glorious solitude
A heavenly presence, gliding in her joy.
But soon a wasting malady began
To prey upon her, frequent in attack,
Yet with such flattering intervals as mock
The hopes of anxious love, and most of all
The sufferer, self-deceived. During those days
Of treacherous respite, many a time hath he,

Who leaves this record of his friend, drawn back
Into the shadow from her social board,
Because too surely in her cheek he saw
The insidious bloom of death ; and then her smiles
And innocent mirth excited deeper grief
Than when long-look'd-for tidings came at last,
That, all her sufferings ended, she was laid
Amid Madeira's orange groves to rest.
O gentle Emma ! o'er a lovelier form
Than thine, Earth never closed ; nor e'er did Heaven
Receive a purer spirit from the world.

Keswick, 1810.

XIX.

FOR A MONUMENT AT ROLISSA.

TIME has been when Rolissa was a name
Ignoble, by the passing traveller heard
And then forthwith forgotten ; now in war
It is renown'd.   For when to her ally,
In bondage by perfidious France oppress'd,
England sent succour, first within this realm
The fated theatre of their long strife
Confronted, here the hostile nations met.
Laborde took here his stand ; upon yon point
Of Mount Saint Anna was his Eagle fix'd ;
The veteran chief, disposing well all aid
Of height and glen, possess'd the mountain straits
A post whose strength thus mann'd and profited
Seem'd to defy the enemy and make
The vantage of assailing numbers vain.
Here, too, before the sun should bend his course
Adown the slope of heaven, so had their plans
Been timed, he look'd for Loison's army, rich
With spoils from Evora and Beja sack'd.
That hope the British Knight areeding well,
With prompt attack prevented ; and nor strength
Of ground, nor leader's skill, nor discipline
Of soldiers practised in the ways of war,

Avail'd that day against the British arm.
Resisting long, but beaten from their stand,
The French fell back; they join'd their greater host
To suffer fresh defeat, and Portugal
First for Sir Arthur wreathed her laurels here.

XX.

FOR A MONUMENT AT VIMEIRO.

THIS is Vimeiro; yonder stream which flows
Westward through heathery highlands to the sea,
Is call'd Maceira, till of late a name,
Save to the dwellers of this peaceful vale,
Known only to the coasting mariner;
Now in the bloody page of war inscribed.
When to the aid of injured Portugal
Struggling against the intolerable yoke
Of treacherous France, England her old ally,
Long tried and always faithful found, went forth,
The embattled hosts in equal strength array'd,
And equal discipline, encountered here.
Junot, the mock Abrantes, led the French,
And confident of skill so oft approved,
And vaunting many a victory, advanced
Against an untried foe.   But when the ranks
Met in the shock of battle, man to man,
And bayonet to bayonet opposed,
The flower of France cut down along their line,
Fell like ripe grass before the mower's scythe,
For the strong arm and rightful cause prevail'd.
That day deliver'd Lisbon from the yoke,
And babes were taught to bless Sir Arthur's name.

XXI.

AT CORUÑA.

WHEN from these shores the British army first
Boldly advanced into the heart of Spain,
The admiring people who beheld its march
Call'd it " the Beautiful." And surely well
Its proud array, its perfect discipline,
Its ample furniture of war compleat,
Its powerful horse, its men of British mould,
All high in heart and hope, all of themselves
Assured, and in their leaders confident,
Deserved the title. Few short weeks elapsed
Ere hither that disastrous host return'd,
A fourth of all its gallant force consumed
In hasty and precipitate retreat,
Stores treasure and artillery, in the wreck
Left to the fierce pursuer, horse and man
Founder'd, and stiffening on the mountain snows.
But when the exulting enemy approach'd
Boasting that he would drive into the sea
The remnant of the wretched fugitives,
Here ere they reach'd their ships, they turn'd at bay.
Then was the proof of British courage seen ;
Against a foe far overnumbering them,
An insolent foe, rejoicing in pursuit,
Sure of the fruit of victory, whatsoe'er

Might be the fate of battle, here they stood
And their safe embarkation, .. all they sought,
Won manfully.   That mournful day avenged
Their sufferings, and redeem'd their country's name;
And thus Coruña, which in this retreat
Had seen the else indelible reproach
Of England, saw the stain effaced in blood.

XXII.

EPITAPH.

HE who in this unconsecrated ground
Obtain'd a soldier's grave, hath left a name
Which will endure in history: the remains
Of Moore, the British General, rest below.
His early prowess Corsica beheld,
When, at Mozello, bleeding, through the breach
He passed victorious ; the Columbian isles
Then saw him tried ; upon the sandy downs
Of Holland was his riper worth approved ;
And leaving on the Egyptian shores his blood,
He gathered there fresh palms. High in repute
A gallant army last he led to Spain,
In arduous times ; for moving in his strength,
With all his mighty means of war compleat,
The Tyrant Buonaparte bore down all
Before him; and the British Chief beheld,
Where'er he look'd, rout, treason, and dismay,
All sides with all embarrassments beset,
And danger pressing on. Hither he came
Before the far out-numbering hosts of France
Retreating to her ships, and close pursued ;
Nor were there wanting men who counsell'd him
To offer terms, and from the enemy

Purchase a respite to embark in peace,
At price of such abasement,.. even to this,
Brave as they were, by hopelessness subdued.
That shameful counsel Moore, in happy hour
Remembering what was due to England's name,
Refused ; he fought, he conquer'd, and he fell.

XXIII.

TO THE

MEMORY OF PAUL BURRARD,

MORTALLY WOUNDED IN THE BATTLE OF CORUÑA.

MYSTERIOUS are the ways of Providence ! —
Old men who have grown grey in camps, and wish'd,
And pray'd, and sought in battle to lay down
The burthen of their age, have seen the young
Fall round, themselves untouch'd ; and balls beside
The graceless and the unblest head have past,
Harmless as hail, to reach some precious life,
For which clasp'd hands, and supplicating eyes,
Duly at morn and eve were raised to Heaven ;
And, in the depth and loneness of the soul
(Then boding all too truly), midnight prayers
Breathed from an anxious pillow wet with tears.
But blessed, even amid their grief, are they
Who, in the hour of visitation, bow
Beneath the unerring will, and look toward
Their Heavenly Father, merciful as just !
They, while they own his goodness, feel that whom
He chastens, them he loves. The cup he gives,
Shall they not drink it? Therefore doth the draught
Resent of comfort in its bitterness,
And carry healing with it. What but this

Could have sustain'd the mourners who were left.
With life-long yearnings, to remember him
Whose early death this monumental verse
Records ?   For never more auspicious hopes
Were nipt in flower, nor finer qualities
From goodliest fabric of mortality
Divorced, nor virtues worthier to adorn
The world transferr'd to heaven, than when, 'ere time
Had measured him the space of nineteen years,
Paul Burrard on Coruña's fatal field
Received his mortal hurt.   Not unprepared
The heroic youth was found : for in the ways
Of piety had he been trained ; and what
The dutiful child upon his mother's knees
Had learnt, the soldier faithfully observed.
In chamber or in tent, the Book of God
Was his beloved manual ; and his life
Beseem'd the lessons which from thence he drew.
For, gallant as he was, and blithe of heart,
Expert of hand, and keen of eye, and prompt
In intellect, religion was the crown
Of all his noble properties.   When Paul
Was by, the scoffer, self-abased, restrain'd
The license of his speech ; and ribaldry
Before his virtuous presence sate rebuked.
And yet so frank and affable a form
His virtue wore, that wheresoe'er he moved
A sunshine of good-will and cheerfulness
Enliven'd all around.   Oh ! marvel not,
If, in the morning of his fair career,
Which promised all that honour could bestow
On high desert, the youth was summon'd hence !

His soul required no farther discipline,
Pure as it was, and capable of Heaven.
Upon the spot from whence he just had seen
His General borne away, the appointed ball
Reach'd him.   But not on that Gallician ground
Was it his fate, like many a British heart,
To mingle with the soil ; the sea received
His mortal relics, .. to a watery grave
Consign'd so near his native shore, so near
His father's house, that they who loved him best,
Unconscious of its import, heard the gun
Which fired his knell. — Alas ! if it were known,
When, in the strife of nations, dreadful Death
Mows down with indiscriminating sweep·
His thousands ten times told, .. if it were known
What ties are sever'd then, what ripening hopes
Blasted, what virtues in their bloom cut off;
How far the desolating scourge extends ;
How wide the misery spreads ; what hearts beneath
Their grief are broken, or survive to feel
Always the irremediable loss ;
Oh ! who of woman born could bear the thought ?
Who but would join with fervent piety
The prayer that asketh in our time for peace ? —
Nor in our time alone ! — Enable us,
Father which art in heaven ! but to receive
And keep thy word : thy kingdom then should come,
Thy will be done on earth ; the victory
Accomplished over Sin as well as Death,
And the great scheme of Providence fulfill'd.

XXIV.

FOR THE BANKS OF THE DOURO.

CROSSING in unexampled enterprize
This great and perilous stream, the English host
Effected here their landing, on the day
When Soult from Porto with his troops was driven.
No sight so joyful ever had been seen
From Douro's banks, .. not when the mountains sent
Their generous produce down, or homeward fleets
Entered from distant seas their port desired ;
Nor e'er were shouts of such glad mariners
So gladly heard, as then the cannon's peal,
And short sharp strokes of frequent musketry,
By the delivered habitants that hour.
For they who beaten then and routed fled
Before victorious England, in their day
Of triumph, had, like fiends let loose from hell,
Fill'd yon devoted city with all forms
Of horror, all unutterable crimes ;
And vengeance now had reach'd the inhuman race
Accurst.   Oh what a scene did Night behold
Within those rescued walls, when festal fires,
And torches, blazing through the bloody streets,
Stream'd their broad light where horse and man in death
Unheeded lay outstretch'd ! Eyes which had wept
In bitterness so long, shed tears of joy,

And from the broken heart thanksgiving mix'd
With anguish rose to Heaven. Sir Arthur then
Might feel how precious in a righteous cause,
Is victory, how divine the soldier's meed
When grateful nations bless the avenging sword !

XXV.

TALAVERA.

YON wide-extended town, whose roofs and towers
And poplar avenues are seen far off,
In goodly prospect over scatter'd woods
Of dusky ilex, boasts among its sons
Of Mariana's name, . . he who hath made
The splendid story of his country's wars
Through all the European kingdoms known.
Yet in his ample annals thou canst find
No braver battle chronicled, than here
Was waged, when Joseph of the stolen crown,
Against the hosts of England and of Spain
His veteran armies brought.   By veteran chiefs
Captain'd, a formidable force they came,
Full fifty thousand.   Victor led them on,
A man grown grey in arms, nor e'er in aught
Dishonoured, till by this opprobrious cause.
He over rude Alverche's summer stream
Winning his way, made first upon the right
His hot attack, where Spain's raw levies, ranged
In double line, had taken their strong stand
In yonder broken ground, by olive groves
Cover'd and flank'd by Tagus.   Soon from thence,

As one whose practised eye could apprehend
All vantages in war, his troops he drew;
And on this hill, the battle's vital point,
Bore with collected power, outnumbering
The British ranks twice told.   Such fearful odds
Were balanced by Sir Arthur's master mind
And by the British heart.   Twice during night
The fatal spot they storm'd, and twice fell back,
Before the bayonet driven.   Again at morn
They made their fiery onset, and again
Repell'd, again at noon renew'd the strife.
Yet was their desperate perseverance vain,
Where skill by equal skill was countervail'd
And numbers by superior courage foil'd;
And when the second night drew over them
Its sheltering cope, in darkness they retired,
At all points beaten.   Long in the red page
Of war, shall Talavera's famous name
Stand forth conspicuous. While that name endures,
Bear in thy soul, O Spain, the memory
Of all thou suffered'st from perfidious France,
Öf all that England in thy cause achieved.

XXVI.

FOR THE DESERTO DE BUSACO.

READER, thou standest upon holy ground
Which Penitence hath chosen for itself,
And war disturbing the deep solitude
Hath left it doubly sacred.   On these heights
The host of Portugal and England stood,
Arrayed against Massena, when the chief
Proud of Rodrigoo and Almeida won,
Press'd forward, thinking the devoted realm
Full sure should fall a prey.   He in his pride
Scorn'd the poor numbers of the English foe,
And thought the children of the land would fly
From his advance, like sheep before the wolf,
Scattering, and lost in terror.   Ill he knew
The Lusitanian spirit !   Ill he knew
The arm, the heart of England !   Ill he knew
Her Wellington !   He learnt to know them here.
That spirit and that arm, that heart, that mind,
Here on Busaco gloriously display'd,
When hence repulsed the beaten boaster wound
Below, his course circuitous, and left
His thousands for the beasts and ravenous fowl.
The Carmelite who in his cell recluse
Was wont to sit, and from a skull receive
Death's silent lesson, whereso'er he walk

Henceforth may find his teachers.   He shall find
The Frenchmen's bones in glen and grove, on rock
And height, where'er the wolves and carrion birds
Have strewn them, wash'd in torrents, bare and bleach'd
By sun and rain and by the winds of heaven.

XXVII.

FOR THE LINES OF TORRES VEDRAS.

THROUGH all Iberia, from the Atlantic shores
To far Pyrene, Wellington hath left
His trophies; but no monument records
To after-time a more enduring praise,
Than this which marks his triumph here attain'd
By intellect, and patience to the end
Holding through good and ill its course assign'd,
The stamp and seal of greatness.   Here the chief
Perceived in foresight Lisbon's sure defence,
A vantage ground for all reverse prepared,
Where Portugal and England might defy
All strength of hostile numbers.   Not for this
Of hostile enterprize did he abate,
Or gallant purpose : witness the proud day
Which saw Soult's murderous host from Porto driven ;
Bear witness Talavera, made by him
Famous for ever ; and that later fight
When from Busaco's solitude the birds,
Then first affrighted in their sanctuary,
Fled from the thunders and the fires of war.
But when Spain's feeble counsels, in delay
As erring, as in action premature,
Had left him in the field without support,
And Buonaparte having trampled down

The strength and pride of Austria, this way turn'd
His single thought and undivided power,
Retreating hither the great General came;
And proud Massena, when the boastful chief
Of plundered Lisbon dreamt, here found himself
Stopt suddenly in his presumptuous course.
From Ericeyra on the western sea,
By Mafra's princely convent, and the heights
Of Montichique, and Bucellas famed
For generous vines, the formidable works
Extending, rested on the guarded shores
Of Tagus, that rich river who received
Into his ample and rejoicing port,
The harvests and the wealth of distant lands,
Secure, insulting with the glad display
The robber's greedy sight. Five months the foe
Beheld these lines, made inexpugnable
By perfect skill, and patriot feelings here
With discipline conjoin'd, courageous hands,
True spirits, and one comprehensive mind
All overseeing and pervading all.
Five months, tormenting still his heart with hope,
He saw his projects frustrated; the power
Of the blaspheming tyrant whom he served
Fail in the proof; his thousands disappear,
In silent and inglorious war consumed;
Till hence retreating, madden'd with despite,
Here did the self-styled Son of Victory leave,
Never to be redeem'd, that vaunted name.

XXVIII.

AT SANTAREM.

FOUR months Massena had his quarters here,
When by those lines deterr'd where Wellington
Defied the power of France, but loth to leave
Rich Lisbon yet unsack'd, he kept his ground,
Till from impending famine, and the force
Array'd in front, and that consuming war
Which still the faithful nation, day and night,
And at all hours was waging on his rear,
He saw no safety, save in swift retreat.
Then of his purpose frustrated, this child
Of Hell, .. so fitlier than of Victory call'd,
Gave his own devilish nature scope, and let
His devilish army loose.   The mournful rolls
That chronicle the guilt of humankind,
Tell not of aught more hideous than the deeds
With which this monster and his kindred troops
Track'd their inhuman way ; all cruelties,
All forms of horror, all deliberate crimes,
Which tongue abhors to utter, ear to hear.
Let this memorial bear Massena's name
For everlasting infamy inscribed.

XXIX.

AT FUENTES D'ONORO.

THE fountains of Onoro which give name
To this poor hamlet, were distain'd with blood,
What time Massena, driven from Portugal
By national virtue in endurance proved,
And England's faithful aid, against the land
Not long delivered, desperately made
His last fierce effort here.   That day, bestreak'd
With slaughter Coa and Agueda ran,
So deeply had the open veins of war
Purpled their mountain feeders.   Strong in means,
With rest, and stores, and numbers reinforced,
Came the ferocious enemy, and ween'd
Beneath their formidable cavalry
To trample down resistance.   But there fought
Against them here, with Britons side by side,
The children of regenerate Portugal,
And their own crimes, and all-beholding Heaven.
Beaten, and hopeless thenceforth of success
The inhuman Marshal, never to be named
By Lusitanian lips without a curse
Of clinging infamy, withdrew and left
These Fountains famous for his overthrow.

XXX.

AT BARROSA.

THOUGH the four quarters of the world have seen
The British valour proved triumphantly
Upon the French, in many a field far-famed,
Yet may the noble Island in her rolls
Of glory write Barrosa's name. For there,
Not by the issue of deliberate plans
Consulted well, was the fierce conflict won,
Nor by the leader's eye intuitive,
Nor force of either arm of war, nor art
Of skill'd artillerist, nor the discipline
Of troops to absolute obedience train'd ;
But by the spring and impulse of the heart,
Brought fairly to the trial, when all else
Seem'd, like a wrestler's garment, thrown aside ;
By individual courage and the sense
Of honour, their old country's, and their own,
There to be forfeited, or there upheld ; ..
This warm'd the soldier's soul, and gave his hand
The strength that carries with it victory.
More to enhance their praise, the day was fought
Against all circumstance ; a painful march,
Through twenty hours of night and day prolong'd,
Forespent the British troops ; and hope delay'd
Had left their spirits pall'd.   But when the word

Was given to turn, and charge, and win the heights;
The welcome order came to them, like rain
Upon a traveller in the thirsty sands.
Rejoicing, up the ascent, and in the front
Of danger, they with steady step advanced,
And with the insupportable bayonet
Drove down the foe.   The vanquished Victor saw
And thought of Talavera, and deplored
His eagle lost.   But England saw well-pleased
Her old ascendency that day sustain'd ;
And Scotland shouting over all her hills,
Among her worthies rank'd another Graham.

XXXI.

FOR A MONUMENT AT ALBUHERA.

SEVEN thousand men lay bleeding on these heights,
When Beresford in strenuous conflict strove
Against a foe whom all the accidents
Of battle favoured, and who knew full well
To seize all offers that occasion gave.
Wounded or dead, seven thousand here were stretch'd,
And on the plain around a myriad more,
Spaniard and Briton and true Portugueze,
Alike approved that day ; and in the cause
Of France, with her flagitious sons compell'd,
Pole and Italian, German, Hollander,
Men of all climes and countries, hither brought,
Doing and suffering, for the work of war.
This point by her superior cavalry
France from the Spaniard won, the elements
Aiding her powerful efforts ; here awhile
She seem'd to rule the conflict ; and from hence
The British and the Lusitanian arm
Dislodged with irresistible assault
The enemy, even when he deem'd the day
Was written for his own.   But not for Soult,

But not for France was that day in the rolls
Of war to be inscribed by Victory's hand,
Not for the inhuman chief, and cause unjust;
She wrote for aftertimes in blood the names
Of Spain and England, Blake and Beresford.

XXXII.

TO THE MEMORY OF SIR WILLIAM MYERS.

SPANIARD or Portugueze! tread reverently
Upon a soldier's grave; no common heart
Lies mingled with the clod beneath thy feet.
To honours and to ample wealth was Myers
In England born; but leaving friends beloved,
And all allurements of that happy land,
His ardent spirit to the field of war
Impell'd him. Fair was his career. He faced
The perils of that memorable day,
When through the iron shower and fiery storm
Of death, the dauntless host of Britain made
Their landing at Aboukir; then not less
Illustrated, than when great Nelson's hand,
As if insulted Heaven with its own wrath   [fleet,
Had arm'd him, smote the miscreant Frenchmen's
And with its wreck wide-floating many a league
Strew'd the rejoicing shores. What then his youth
Held forth of promise, amply was confirm'd
When Wellesley, upon Talavera's plain,
On the mock monarch won his coronet:
There when the trophies of the field were reap'd
Was he for gallant bearing eminent
When all did bravely. But his valour's orb
Shone brightest at its setting. On the field

Of Albuhera he the fusileers
Led to regain the heights, and promised them
A glorious day; a glorious day was given;
The heights were gain'd, the victory was achieved,
And Myers received from death his deathless crown.
Here to Valverde was he borne, and here
His faithful men amid this olive grove,
The olive emblem here of endless peace,
Laid him to rest.   Spaniard or Portugueze,
In your good cause the British soldier fell;
Tread reverently upon his honour'd grave.

XXXIII.

EPITAPH.

STEEP is the soldier's path ; nor are the heights
Of glory to be won without long toil
And arduous efforts of enduring hope ;
Save when Death takes the aspirant by the hand,
And cutting short the work of years, at once
Lifts him to that conspicuous eminence.
Such fate was mine. — The standard of the Buffs
I bore at Albuhera, on that day
When, covered by a shower, and fatally
For friends misdeem'd, the Polish lancers fell
Upon our rear.   Surrounding me, they claim'd
My precious charge. — "Not but with life!" I cried,
And life was given for immortality.
The flag which to my heart I held, when wet
With that heart's blood, was soon victoriously
Regain'd on that great day.   In former times,
Marlborough beheld it borne at Ramilies ;
For Brunswick and for liberty it waved
Triumphant at Culloden ; and hath seen
The lilies on the Caribbean shores
Abased before it.   Then too in the front
Of battle did it flap exultingly,
When Douro, with its wide stream interposed,
Saved not the French invaders from attack,

Discomfiture, and ignominious rout.
My name is Thomas : undisgraced have I
Transmitted it.   He who in days to come
May bear the honour'd banner to the field,
Will think of Albuhera, and of me.

XXXIV.

FOR THE WALLS OF CIUDAD RODRIGO.

HERE Craufurd fell, victorious, in the breach,
Leading his countrymen in that assault
Which won from haughty France these rescued walls
And here intomb'd far from his native land
And kindred dust, his honour'd relics rest.
Well was he versed in war, in the Orient train'd
Beneath Cornwallis; then for many a year
Following through arduous and ill-fated fields
The Austrian banners; on the sea-like shores
Of Plata next, still by malignant stars
Pursued; and in that miserable retreat,
For which Coruña witness'd on her hills
The pledge of vengeance given.   At length he saw,
Long woo'd and well deserved, the brighter face
Of Fortune, upon Coa's banks vouchsafed,
Before Almeida, when Massena found
The fourfold vantage of his numbers foil'd,
Before the Briton, and the Portugal,
There vindicating first his old renown,
And Craufurd's mind that day presiding there.
Again was her auspicious countenance
Upon Busaco's holy heights reveal'd;
And when by Torres Vedras, Wellington,
Wisely secure, defied the boastful French,

With all their power ; and when Onoro's springs
Beheld that execrable enemy
Again chastised beneath the avenging arm.
Too early here his honourable course
He closed, and won his noble sepulchre.
Where should the soldier rest so worthily
As where he fell ?   Be thou his monument,
O City of Rodrigo, yea be thou,
To latest time, his trophy and his tomb!
Sultans, or Pharaohs of the elder world,
Lie not in Mosque or Pyramid enshrined
Thus gloriously, nor in so proud a grave.

XXXV.

TO THE MEMORY OF MAJOR GENERAL MACKINNON.

Son of an old and honourable house,
Henry Mackinnon from the Hebrides
Drew his descent, but upon English ground
An English mother bore him.   Dauphiny
Beheld the blossom of his opening years;
For hoping in that genial clime to save
A child of feebler frame, his parents there
Awhile their sojourn fix'd : and thus it chanced
That in that generous season, when the heart
Yet from the world is pure and undefiled,
Napoleon Buonaparte was his friend.
The adventurous Corsican, like Henry, then
Young, and a stranger in the land of France,
Their frequent and their favour'd guest became,
Finding a cheerful welcome at all hours,
Kindness, esteem, and in the English youth
Quick sympathy of apprehensive mind
And lofty thought heroic.   On the way
Of life they parted, not to meet again.
Each follow'd war, but, oh ! how differently
Did the two spirits which till now had grown
Like two fair plants, it seem'd, of kindred seed,
Develope in that awful element !

For never had benignant nature shower'd
More bounteously than on Mackinnon's head
Her choicest gifts. Form, features, intellect,
Were such as might at once command and win
All hearts. In all relationships approved,
Son, brother, husband, father, friend, his life
Was beautiful ; and when in tented fields,
Such as the soldier should be in the sight
Of God and man was he. Poor praise it were
To speak his worth evinced upon the banks
Of Douro, Talavera's trophied plain,
Busaco's summit, and what other days,
Many and glorious all, illustrated
His bright career. Worthier of him to say
That in the midst of camps his manly breast
Retain'd its youthful virtue ; that he walk'd
Through blood and evil uncontaminate,
And that the stern necessity of war
But nurtured with its painful discipline
Thoughtful compassion in that gentle soul,
And feelings such as man should cherish still
For all of woman born. He met his death
When at Rodrigo on the breach he stood
Triumphant ; to a soldier's wish it came
Instant, and in the hour of victory.
Mothers and maids of Portugal, oh bring
Your garlands here, and strew his grave with flowers;
And lead the children to his monument,
Grey-headed sires, for it is holy ground !
For tenderness and valour in his heart,
As in your own Nunalures, had made
Their habitation ; for a dearer life.

Never in battle hath been offered up,
Since in like cause and in unhappy day,
By Zutphen's walls the peerless Sydney fell.
'T is said that Buonaparte, when he heard
How thus among the multitude whose blood
Cries out to Heaven upon his guilty head,
His early friend had fallen, was touch'd with grief.
If aught it may avail him, be that thought,
That brief recurrence of humanity
In his hard heart, remember'd in his hour.

XXXVI.

FOR THE AFFAIR AT ARROYO MOLINOS.

HE who may chronicle Spain's arduous strife
Against the Intruder, hath to speak of fields
Profuselier fed with blood, and victories
Borne wider on the wings of glad report;
Yet shall this town, which from the mill-stream takes
Its humble name, be storied as the spot
Where the vain Frenchman, insolent too long
Of power and of success, first saw the strength
Of England in prompt enterprize essayed,
And felt his fortunes ebb, from that day forth
Swept back upon the refluent tide of war.
Girard lay here, who late from Caceres,
Far as his active cavalry could scour,
Had pillaged and opprest the country round;
The Spaniard and the Portugueze he scorn'd,
And deem'd the British soldiers all too slow,
To seize occasion, unalert in war,
And therefore brave in vain. In such belief
Secure at night he laid him down to sleep,
Nor dreamt that these disparaged enemies
With drum and trumpet should in martial charge
Sound his reveille. All day their march severe
They held through wind and drenching rain; all night
The autumnal tempest unabating raged,

While in their comfortless and open camp
They cheer'd themselves with patient hope: the storm
Was their ally, and moving in the mist,
When morning open'd, on the astonish'd foe
They burst. Soon routed horse and foot, the French
On all sides scattering, fled, on every side
Beset, and every where pursued, with loss
Of half their numbers captured, their whole stores,
And all their gathered plunder.   'T was a day
Of surest omen, such as fill'd with joy
True English hearts... No happier peals have e'er
Been roll'd abroad from town and village tower
Than gladden'd then with their exultant sound
Salopian vales ; and flowing cups were brimm'd
All round the Wrekin to Sir Rowland's name.

XXXVII.

WRITTEN IN AN UNPUBLISHED VOLUME OF LETTERS
AND MISCELLANEOUS PAPERS, BY BARRÉ CHARLES
ROBERTS.

NOT often hath the cold insensate earth
Closed over such fair hopes, as when the grave
Received young Barré's perishable part;
Nor death destroyed so sweet a dream of life.
Nature, who sometimes lavisheth her gifts
With fatal bounty, had conferred on him
Even such endowments as parental love
Might in its wisest prayer have ask'd of Heaven;
An intellect that, choosing for itself
The better part, went forth into the fields
Of knowledge, and with never-sated thirst
Drank of the living springs; a judgement calm
And clear; a heart affectionate; a soul
Within whose quiet sphere, no vanities
Or low desires had place. Nor were the seeds
Of excellence thus largely given, and left
To struggle with impediment of clime
Austere, or niggard soil; all circumstance
Of happy fortune was to him vouchsafed;
His way of life was as through garden-walks

Wherein no thorns are seen, save such as grow,
Types of our human state, with fruits and flowers.
In all things favoured thus auspiciously,
But in his father most.   An intercourse
So beautiful no former record shows
In such relationship displayed, where through
Familiar friendship's perfect confidence,
The father's ever-watchful tenderness
Meets ever in the son's entire respect
Its due return devout, and playful love
Mingles with every thing, and sheds o'er all
A sunshine of its own.   Should we then say
The parents purchased at too dear a cost
This deep delight, the deepest, purest joy
Which Heaven hath here assign'd us, when they saw
Their child of hope, just in the May of life,
Beneath a slow and cankering malady,
With irremediable decay consumed,
Sink to the untimely grave?   Oh, think not thus !
Nor deem that such long anguish, and the grief
Which in the inmost soul doth strike its roots
There to abide through time, can overweigh
The blessings which have been, and yet shall be !
Think not that He in Whom we live, doth mock
Our dearest aspirations !   Think not love,
Genius, and virtue should inhere alone
In mere mortality, and Earth put out
The sparks which are of Heaven !   We are not left
In darkness, nor devoid of hope.   The Light
Of Faith hath risen to us : the vanquish'd **Grave**
To us the great consolatory truth

Proclaim'd that He who wounds will heal; and **Death**
Opening the gates of Immortality,
The spirits whom it hath dissevered **here,**
In everlasting union **re-unite.**

Keswick, 1814.

XXXVIII.

EPITAPH.

TIME and the world, whose magnitude and weight
Bear on us in this Now, and hold us here
To earth enthrall'd, . . what are they in the Past?
And in the prospect of the immortal Soul
How poor a speck! Not here her resting-place,
Her portion is not here; and happiest they
Who, gathering early all that Earth can give,
Shake off its mortal coil, and speed for Heaven.
Such fate had he whose relics moulder here.
Few were his years, but yet enough to teach
Love, duty, generous feelings, high desires,
Faith, hope, devotion: and what more could length
Of days have brought him? What, but vanity,
Joys frailer even than health or human life;
Temptation, sin and sorrow, both too sure,
Evils that wound, and cares that fret the heart.
Repine not, therefore, ye who love the dead.

XXXIX.

EPITAPH.

SOME there will be to whom, as here they read,
While yet these lines are from the chisel sharp,
The name of Clement Francis, will recall
His countenance benign; and some who knew
What stores of knowledge and what humble thoughts
What wise desires, what cheerful piety,
In happy union form'd the character
Which faithfully impress'd his aspect meek.
And others too there are, who in their hearts
Will bear the memory of his worth enshrined,
For tender and for reverential thoughts,
When grief hath had its course, a life-long theme,
A little while, and these, who to the truth
Of this poor tributary strain could bear
Their witness, will themselves have past away,
And this cold marble monument present
Words which can then within no living mind
Create the ideal form they once evoked;
This, then, the sole memorial of the dead.
So be it. Only that which was of earth
Hath perish'd; only that which was infirm,
Mortal, corruptible, and brought with it
The seed connate of death. A place in Time

Is given us, only that we may prepare
Our portion for Eternity : the Soul
Possesseth there what treasures for itself,
Wise to salvation, it laid up in Heaven.
O Man, take thou this lesson from the Grave !
There too all true affections shall revive,
To fade no more ; all losses be restored,
All griefs be heal'd, all holy hopes fulfill'd.

INSCRIPTIONS

FOR THE CALEDONIAN CANAL.

XL.

1. AT CLACHNACHARRY.

ATHWART the island here, from sea to sea,
Between these mountain barriers, the Great Glen
Of Scotland offers to the traveller,
Through wilds impervious else, an easy path,
Along the shore of rivers and of lakes,
In line continuous, whence the waters flow
Dividing east and west.   Thus had they held
For untold centuries their perpetual course
Unprofited, till in the Georgian age
This mighty work was plann'd, which should unite
The lakes, control the innavigable streams,
And through the bowels of the land deduce
A way, where vessels which must else have braved
The formidable Cape, and have essayed
The perils of the Hyperborean Sea,
Might from the Baltic to the Atlantic deep
Pass and repass at will.   So when the storm

M 2

Careers abroad, may they securely here,
Through birchen groves, green fields, and pastoral
        hills,
Pursue their voyage home.   Humanity
May boast this proud expenditure, begun
By Britain in a time of arduous war;
Through all the efforts and emergencies
Of that long strife continued, and achieved
After her triumph, even at the time
When national burdens bearing on the state
Were felt with heaviest pressure.   Such expense
Is best economy.   In growing wealth,
Comfort, and spreading industry, behold
The fruits immediate ! And, in days to come,
Fitly shall this great British work be named
With whatsoe'er of most magnificence
For public use, Rome in her plenitude
Of power effected, or all-glorious Greece,
Or Egypt, mother-land of all the arts.

XLI.

2. AT FORT AUGUSTUS.

THOU who hast reach d this level where the glede,
Wheeling between the mountains in mid air,
Eastward or westward as his gyre inclines,
Descries the German or the Atlantic Sea,
Pause here ; and, as thou seest the ship pursue
Her easy way serene, call thou to mind
By what exertions of victorious art
The way was open'd.   Fourteen times upheaved,
The vessel hath ascended, since she changed
The salt sea water for the highland lymph ;
As oft in imperceptible descent
Must, step by step, be lower'd, before she woo
The ocean breeze again.   Thou hast beheld
What basins, most capacious of their kind,
Enclose her, while the obedient element
Lifts or depones its burthen.   Thou hast seen
The torrent hurrying from its native hills
Pass underneath the broad canal inhumed,
Then issue harmless thence ; the rivulet
Admitted by its intake peaceably,
Forthwith by gentle overfall discharged :
And haply too thou hast observed the herds
Frequent their vaulted path, unconscious they
That the wide waters on the long low arch

Above them, lie sustained.   What other works
Science, audacious in emprize, hath wrought,
Meet not the eye, but well may fill the mind.
Not from the bowels of the land alone,
From lake and stream hath their diluvial wreck
Been scoop'd to form this navigable way;
Huge rivers were controll'd, or from their course
Shoulder'd aside; and at the eastern mouth,
Where the salt ooze denied a resting place,
There were the deep foundations laid, by weight
On weight immersed, and pile on pile down-driven,
Till steadfast as the everlasting rocks,
The massive outwork stands.   Contemplate now
What days and nights of thought, what years of toil,
What inexhaustive springs of public wealth
The vast design required; the immediate good,
The future benefit progressive still;
And thou wilt pay thy tribute of due praise
To those whose counsels, whose decrees, whose care,
For after ages formed the generous work.

XLII.

3. AT BANAVIE.

WHERE these capacious basins, by the laws
Of the subjacent element receive
The ship, descending or upraised, eight times,
From stage to stage with unfelt agency
Translated ; fitliest may the marble here
Record the Architect's immortal name.
Telford it was, by whose presiding mind
The whole great work was plann'd and perfected ;
Telford, who o'er the vale of Cambrian Dee,
Aloft in air, at giddy height upborne,
Carried his navigable road, and hung
High o'er Menaï's straits the bending bridge ;
Structures of more ambitious enterprize
Than minstrels in the age of old romance
To their own Merlin's magic lore ascribed.
Nor hath he for his native land perform'd
Less in this proud design ; and where his piers
Around her coast from many a fisher's creek
Unshelter'd else, and many an ample port,
Repel the assailing storm ; and where his roads
In beautiful and sinuous line far seen,
Wind with the vale, and win the long ascent,
Now o'er the deep morass sustain d, and now
Across ravine, or glen, or estuary,
Opening a passage through the wilds subdued.

XLIII.

EPITAPH IN BUTLEIGH CHURCH.

DIVIDED far by death were they, whose names
In honour here united, as in birth,
This monumental verse records.   They drew
In Dorset's healthy vales their natal breath,
And from these shores beheld the ocean first,
Whereon in early youth, with one accord
They chose their way of fortune; to that course
By Hood and Bridport's bright example drawn,
Their kinsmen, children of this place, and sons
Of one, who in his faithful ministry
Inculcated within these hallowed walls
The truths in mercy to mankind reveal'd.
Worthy were these three brethren each to add
New honours to the already honour'd name
But Arthur, in the morning of his day,
Perish'd amid the Caribbean sea,
When the Pomona, by a hurricane
Whirl'd, riven and overwhelmed, with all her crew
Into the deep went down.   A longer date
To Alexander was assign'd, for hope,
For fair ambition, and for fond regret,
Alas, how short! for duty, for desert,
Sufficing; and, while Time preserves the roll
Of Britain's naval feats, for good report.

A boy, with Cook he rounded the great globe ;
A youth, in many a celebrated fight
With Rodney had his part ; and having reach'd
Life's middle stage, engaging ship to ship,
When the French Hercules, a gallant foe,
Struck to the British Mars his three-striped flag,
He fell, in the moment of his victory.
Here his remains in sure and certain hope
Are laid, until the hour when Earth and Sea
Shall render up their dead.   One brother yet
Survived, with Keppel and with Rodney train'd
In battles, with the Lord of Nile approved,
Ere in command he worthily upheld
Old England's high prerogative.   In the east,
The west, the Baltic and the Midland seas,
Yea, wheresoever hostile fleets have plough'd
The ensanguined deep, his thunders have been heard,
His flag in brave defiance hath been seen ;
And bravest enemies at Sir Samuel's name
Felt fatal presage in their inmost heart,
Of unavertible defeat foredoom'd.
Thus in the path of glory he rode on,
Victorious alway, adding praise to praise ;
Till full of honours, not of years, beneath
The venom of the infected clime he sunk,
On Coromandel's coast, completing there
His service, only when his life was spent.

To the three brethren, Alexander's son
(Sole scion he in whom their line survived),
With English feeling, and the deeper sense
Of filial duty, consecrates this tomb.

1827.

XLIV.

EPITAPH.

To Butler's venerable memory
By private gratitude for public worth
This monument is raised, here where twelve years
Meekly the blameless Prelate exercised
His pastoral charge ; and whither, though removed
A little while to Durham's wider See,
His mortal relics were conveyed to rest.
Born in dissent, and in the school of schism
Bred, he withstood the withering influence
Of that unwholesome nurture.   To the Church,
In strength of mind mature and judgement clear,
A convert, in sincerity of heart
Seeking the truth, deliberately convinced,
And finding there the truth he sought, he came.
In honour must his high desert be held
While there is any virtue, any praise ;
For he it was whose gifted intellect
First apprehended, and developed first
The analogy connate, which in its course
And constitution Nature manifests
To the Creator's word and will divine ;
And in the depth of that great argument
Laying his firm foundation, built thereon

Proofs never to be shaken of the truths
Reveal'd from Heaven in mercy to mankind;
Allying thus Philosophy with Faith,
And finding in things seen and known, the type
And evidence of those within the veil.

XLV.

DEDICATION OF THE AUTHOR'S COLLOQUIES ON THE PROGRESS AND PROSPECTS OF SOCIETY.

TO

THE MEMORY OF THE REVEREND HERBERT HILL,

Formerly Student of Christ Church, Oxford : successively Chaplain to the
British Factories at Porto and at Lisbon ; and late Rector of Streatham ;
who was released from this life, Sept. 19. 1828, in the 80th year of his age.

NOT upon marble or sepulchral brass
Have I the record of thy worth inscribed,
Dear Uncle ! nor from Chantrey's chisel ask'd
A monumental statue, which might wear
Through many an age thy venerable form.
Such tribute, were I rich in this world's wealth,
Should rightfully be rendered, in discharge
Of grateful duty, to the world evinced
When testifying so by outward sign
Its deep and inmost sense.   But what I can
Is rendered piously, prefixing here
Thy perfect lineaments, two centuries
Before thy birth by Holbein's happy hand
Prefigured thus.   It is the portraiture
Of More, the mild, the learned, and the good ;
Traced in that better stage of human life,

When vain imaginations, troublous thoughts,
And hopes and fears have had their course, and left
The intellect composed, the heart at rest,
Nor yet decay hath touch'd our mortal frame.
Such was the man whom Henry, of desert
Appreciant alway, chose for highest trust;
Whom England in that eminence approved;
Whom Europe honoured, and Erasmus loved.
Such was he ere heart-hardening bigotry
Obscured his spirit, made him with himself
Discordant, and contracting then his brow,
With sour defeature marr'd his countenance.
What he was, in his best and happiest time,
Even such wert thou, dear Uncle! such thy look
Benign and thoughtful; such thy placid mien;
Thine eye serene, significant and strong,
Bright in its quietness, yet brightening oft
With quick emotion of benevolence,
Or flash of active fancy, and that mirth
Which aye with sober wisdom well accords.
Nor ever did true Nature, with more nice
Exactitude, fit to the inner man
The fleshly mould, than when she stampt on thine
Her best credentials, and bestow'd on thee
An aspect, to whose sure benignity
Beasts with instinctive confidence could trust,
Which at a glance obtain'd respect from men,
And won at once good will from all the good.

Such as in semblance, such in word and deed
Lisbon beheld him, when for many a year
The even tenour of his spotless life

Adorn'd the English Church, . . her minister
In that strong hold of Rome's Idolatry,
To God and man approved.   What Englishman,
Who in those peaceful days of Portugal
Resorted thither, curious to observe
Her cities, and the works and ways of men,
But sought him, and from his abundant stores
Of knowledge profited ?   What stricken one,
Sent thither to protract a living death,
Forlorn perhaps, and friendless else, but found
A friend in him ?   What mourners, . .who had seen
The object of their agonizing hopes
In that sad cypress ground deposited
Wherein so many a flower of British growth,
Untimely faded and cut down, is laid,
In foreign earth compress'd, . . but bore away
A life-long sense of his compassionate care,
His Christian goodness?   Faithful shepherd he,
And vigilant against the wolves, who there,
If entrance might be won, would straight beset
The dying stranger, and with merciless zeal
Bay the death-bed.   In every family
Throughout his fold was he the welcome guest,
Alike to every generation dear,
The children's favourite, and the grandsire's friend ;
Tried, trusted and beloved.   So liberal too
In secret alms, even to his utmost means,
That they who served him, and who saw in part
The channels where his constant bounty ran,
Maugre their own uncharitable faith,
Believed him, for his works, secure of Heaven.

It would have been a grief for me to think
The features, which so perfectly express'd
That excellent mind, should irretrievably
From earth have past away, existing now
Only in some few faithful memories
Insoul'd, and not by any limner's skill
To be imbodied thence.   A blessing then
On him, in whose prophetic counterfeit
Preserved, the children now, who were the crown
Of his old age, may see their father's face,
Here to the very life pourtray'd, as when
Spain's mountain passes, and her ilex woods,
And fragrant wildernesses, side by side,
With him I traversed, in my morn of youth,
And gather'd knowledge from his full discourse.
Often in former years I pointed out,
Well-pleased, the casual portrait, which so well
Assorted in all points; and haply since,
While lingering o'er this meditative work,
Sometimes that likeness, not unconsciously,
Hath tinged the strain; and therefore, for the sake
Of this resemblance, are these volumes now
Thus to his memory properly inscribed.

O friend! O more than father! whom I found
Forbearing alway, alway kind; to whom
No gratitude can speak the debt I owe;
Far on their earthly pilgrimage advanced
Are they who knew thee when we drew the breath
Of that delicious clime! The most are gone;
And whoso yet survive of those who then
Were in their summer season, on the tree

Of life hang here and there like wintry leaves,
Which the first breeze will from the bough bring
    down.
I, too, am in the sear, the yellow leaf.
And yet, (no wish is nearer to my heart,)
One arduous labour more, as unto thee
In duty bound, full fain would I complete,
(So Heaven permit,) recording faithfully
The heroic rise, the glories, the decline,
Of that fallen country, dear to us, wherein
The better portion of thy days was past ;
And, where, in fruitful intercourse with thee,
My intellectual life received betimes
The bias it hath kept.   Poor Portugal,
In us thou harbouredst no ungrateful guests !
We loved thee well ; Mother magnanimous
Of mighty intellects and faithful hearts, . .
For such in other times thou wert, nor yet
To be despair'd of, for not yet, methinks,
Degenerate wholly, . . yes, we loved thee well !
And in thy moving story, (so but life
Be given me to mature the gathered store
Of thirty years,) poet and politick,
And Christian sage, (only philosopher
Who from the Well of living water drinks
Never to thirst again,) shall find, I ween,
For fancy, and for profitable thought,
Abundant food.
                Alas! should this be given,
Such consummation of my work will now
Be but a mournful close, the one being gone,
Whom to have satisfied was still to me

A pure reward, outweighing far all breath
Of public praise. O friend revered, O guide
And fellow-labourer in this ample field,
How large a portion of myself hath past
With thee, from earth to Heaven!.. Thus they who
    reach
Grey hairs die piecemeal. But in good old age
Thou hast departed; not to be bewail'd, ..
Oh no! The promise on the Mount vouchsafed,
Nor abrogate by any later law
Reveal'd to man,.. that promise, as by thee
Full piously deserved, was faithfully
In thee fulfill'd, and in the land thy days
Were long. I would not, as I saw thee last,
For a king's ransom, have detain'd thee here, ..
Bent, like the antique sculptor's limbless trunk,
By chronic pain, yet with thine eye unquench'd,
The ear undimm'd, the mind retentive still,
The heart unchanged, the intellectual lamp
Burning in its corporeal sepulchre.
No; not if human wishes had had power
To have suspended Nature's constant work,
Would they who loved thee have detain'd thee thus,
Waiting for death.
              That trance is over. Thou
Art enter'd on thy heavenly heritage;
And I, whose dial of mortality
Points to the eleventh hour, shall follow soon.
Meantime, with dutiful and patient hope,
I labour that our names conjoin'd may long
Survive, in honour one day to be held
Where old Lisboa from her hills o'erlooks

Expanded Tagus, with its populous shores
And pine woods, to Palmella's crested height:
Nor there alone ; but in those rising realms
Where now the offsets of the Lusian tree
Push forth their vigorous shoots, . . from central
        plains,
Whence rivers flow divergent, to the gulph
Southward, where wild Parana disembogues
A sea-like stream ; and northward, in a world
Of forests, where huge Orellana clips
His thousand islands with his thousand arms.

CARMEN TRIUMPHALE,

FOR THE COMMENCEMENT OF THE YEAR

1814.

Illi justitiam confirmavere triumphi,
Præsentes docuere Deos.
CLAUDIAN.

CARMEN TRIUMPHALE,

FOR THE COMMENCEMENT OF THE YEAR
1814.

1.

In happy hour doth he receive
The Laurel, meed of famous Bards of yore,
Which Dryden and diviner Spenser wore, . .
In happy hour, and well may he rejoice,
Whose earliest task must be
To raise the exultant hymn for victory,
And join a nation's joy with harp and voice,
Pouring the strain of triumph on the wind,
Glory to God, his song, Deliverance for Mankind!

II.

Wake, lute and harp! My soul take up the strain!
Glory to God! Deliverance for Mankind!
Joy. . . for all Nations, joy! But most for thee,
Who hast so nobly fill'd thy part assign'd,
O England! O my glorious native land!
For thou in evil days didst stand
Against leagued Europe all in arms array'd,
Single and undismay'd,
Thy hope in Heaven and in thine own right hand.
Now are thy virtuous efforts overpaid,

Thy generous counsels now their guerdon find,
Glory to God ! Deliverance for Mankind !

III.

Dread was the strife, for mighty was the foe
Who sought with his whole strength thy overthrow.
The Nations bow'd before him ; some in war
Subdued, some yielding to superior art ;
Submiss, they follow'd his victorious car.
Their Kings, like Satraps, waited round his throne ;
For Britain's ruin and their own,
By force or fraud in monstrous league combined.
Alone, in that disastrous hour,
Britain stood firm and braved his power ;
Alone she fought the battles of mankind.

IV.

O virtue which, above all former fame,
Exalts her venerable name !
O joy of joys for every British breast !
That with that mighty peril full in view,
The Queen of Ocean to herself was true !
That no weak heart, no abject mind possess'd
Her counsels, to abase her lofty crest, . .
(Then had she sunk in everlasting shame,)
But ready still to succour the oppress'd,
Her Red Cross floated on the waves unfurl'd,
Offering Redemption to the groaning world.

V.

First from his trance the heroic Spaniard woke ;
His chains he broke,

And casting off his neck the treacherous yoke,
He call'd on England, on his generous foe :
For well he knew that wheresoe'er
Wise policy prevail'd, or brave despair,
Thither would Britain's liberal succours flow,
Her arm be present there.
Then, too, regenerate Portugal display'd
Her ancient virtue, dormant all-too-long.
Rising against intolerable wrong,
On England, on her old ally, for aid
The faithful nation call'd in her distress :
And well that old ally the call obey'd,
Well was that faithful friendship then repaid.

VI.

Say from thy trophied field how well,
Vimeiro ! Rocky Douro tell !
And thou, Busaco, on whose sacred height
The astonished Carmelite,
While those unwonted thunders shook his cell,
Join'd with his prayers the fervour of the fight.
Bear witness those Old Towers, where many a day
Waiting with foresight calm the fitting hour,
The Wellesley, gathering strength in wise delay,
Defied the Tyrant's undivided power.
Swore not the boastful Frenchman in his might,
Into the sea to drive his Island-foe ?
Tagus and Zezere, in secret night,
Ye saw that host of ruffians take their flight !
And in the Sun's broad light
Onoro's Springs beheld their overthrow.

N 4

VII.

Patient of loss, profuse of life,
Meantime had Spain endured the strife ;
And though she saw her cities yield,
Her armies scatter'd in the field,
Her strongest bulwarks fall;
The danger undismay'd she view'd,
Knowing that nought could e'er appal
The Spaniards' fortitude.
What though the Tyrant, drunk with power,
Might vaunt himself, in impious hour,
Lord and Disposer of this earthly ball ?
Her cause is just, and Heaven is over all.

VIII.

Therefore no thought of fear debased
Her judgement, nor her acts disgraced.
To every ill, but not to shame resign'd,
All sufferings, all calamities she bore.
She bade the people call to mind
Their heroes of the days of yore,
Pelayo and the Campeador,
With all who once in battle strong,
Lived still in story and in song.
Against the Moor, age after age,
Their stubborn warfare did they wage ;
Age after age, from sire to son,
The hallowed sword was handed down ;
Nor did they from that warfare cease,
And sheathe that hallowed sword in peace,
Until the work was done.

IX.

Thus, in the famous days of yore,
Their fathers triumph'd o'er the Moor.
They gloried in his overthrow,
But touch'd not with reproach his gallant name;
For fairly, and with hostile aim profest,
The Moor had rear'd his haughty crest,
An open, honourable foe;
But as a friend the treacherous Frenchman came,
And Spain received him as a guest.
Think what your fathers were! she cried,
Think what ye are, in sufferings tried;
And think of what your sons must be . .
Even as ye make them . . slaves or free!

X.

Strains such as these from Spain's three seas,
And from the farthest Pyrenees,
Rung through the region. Vengeance was the word
One impulse to all hearts at once was given;
From every voice the sacred cry was heard,
And borne abroad by all the winds of Heaven.
Heaven too, to whom the Spaniards look'd for aid,
A spirit equal to the hour bestow'd;
And gloriously the debt they paid,
Which to their valiant ancestors they owed;
And gloriously against the power of France
Maintain'd their children's proud inheritance.
Their steady purpose no defeat could move,
No horrors could abate their constant mind;
Hope had its source and resting place above,
And they, to loss of all on earth resign'd,

Suffer'd, to save their country, and mankind.
What strain heroic might suffice to tell,
How Zaragoza stood, and how she fell?
Ne'er since yon sun began his daily round,
Was higher virtue, holier valour, found.
Than on that consecrated ground.

XI.

Alone the noble Nation stood,
When from Coruña, in the main,
The star of England set in blood.
Ere long on Talavera's plain,
That star resplendent rose again;
And though that day was doom'd to be
A day of frustrate victory,
Not vainly bled the brave;
For French and Spaniard there might see
That England's arm was strong to save;
Fair promise there the Wellesley gave,
And well in sight of Earth and Heaven,
Did he redeem the pledge which there was given.

XII.

Lord of Conquest, heir of Fame,
From rescued Portugal he came.
Rodrigo's walls in vain oppose;
In vain thy bulwarks, Badajoz;
And Salamanca's heights proclaim
The Conqueror's praise, the Wellesley's name.
Oh, had the sun stood still that hour,
When Marmont and his broken power
Fled from their field of shame!

Spain felt through all her realms the electric blow
    Cadiz in peace expands her gates again ;
    And Betis, who to bondage long resign'd,
    Flow'd mournfully along the silent plain,
        Into her joyful bosom unconfined,
Receives once more the treasures of the main.

XIII.

What now shall check the Wellesley, when at length
    Onward he goes, rejoicing in his strength ?
    From Douro, from Castille's extended plain,
        The foe, a numerous band,
    Retire ; amid the heights which overhang
Dark Ebro's bed, they think to make their stand.
He reads their purpose, and prevents their speed ;
        And still as they recede,
    Impetuously he presses on their way ;
    Till by Vittoria's walls they stood at bay,
    And drew their battle up in fair array.

XIV.

        Vain their array, their valour vain :
    There did the practised Frenchman find
        A master arm, a master mind !
        Behold his veteran army driven
    Like dust before the breath of Heaven,
    Like leaves before the autumnal wind !
Now, Britain, now thy brow with laurels bind ;
Raise now the song of joy for rescued Spain !
And Europe, take thou up the awakening strain . .
    Glory to God ! Deliverance for mankind !

XV.

From Spain the living spark went forth:
The flame hath caught, the flame is spread !
It warms, . . it fires the farthest North.
Behold ! the awaken'd Moscovite
Meets the Tyrant in his might ;
The Brandenburg, at Freedom's call,
Rises more glorious from his fall ;
And Frederic, best and greatest of the name,
Treads in the path of duty and of fame.
See Austria from her painful trance awake !
The breath of God goes forth,..the dry bones shake!
Up Germany ! . . with all thy nations rise !
Land of the virtuous and the wise,
No longer let that free, that mighty mind,
Endure its shame ! She rose as from the dead,
She broke her chains upon the oppressor's head ..
Glory to God ! Deliverance for Mankind !

XVI.

Open thy gates, O Hanover ! display
Thy loyal banners to the day ;
Receive thy old illustrious line once more !
Beneath an Upstart's yoke opprest,
Long hath it been thy fortune to deplore
That line, whose fostering and paternal sway
So many an age thy grateful children blest.
The yoke is broken now :.. A mightier hand
Hath dash'd, .. in pieces dash'd, .. the iron rod.
To meet her Princes, the deliver'd land
Pours her rejoicing multitudes abroad ;
The happy bells, from every town and tower,

Roll their glad peals upon the joyful wind ;
And from all hearts and tongues, with one consent,
The high thanksgiving strain to heaven is sent, . .
    Glory to God ! Deliverance for Mankind !

XVII.

Egmont and Horn, heard ye that holy cry,
Martyrs of Freedom, from your seats in Heaven ?
And William the Deliverer, doth thine eye
    Regard from yon empyreal realm the land
        For which thy blood was given ?
What ills hath that poor Country suffer'd long !
Deceived, despised, and plunder'd, and oppress'd,
    Mockery and insult aggravating wrong !
    Severely she her errors hath atoned,
        And long in anguish groan'd,
Wearing the patient semblance of despair,
While fervent curses rose with every prayer,
In mercy Heaven at length its ear inclined ;
The avenging armies of the North draw nigh,
    Joy for the injured Hollander ! . . the cry
        Of Orange rends the sky !
All hearts are now in one good cause combined, .
Once more that flag triumphant floats on high, . .
    Glory to God ! Deliverance for Mankind !

XVIII.

When shall the Dove go forth ? Oh when
Shall Peace return among the Sons of Men ?
Hasten benignant Heaven the blessed day !
    Justice must go before,
And Retribution must make plain the way ;

Force must be crushed by Force,
The power of Evil by the power of Good,
Ere Order bless the suffering world once more,
Or Peace return again.
Hold then right on in your auspicious course,
Ye Princes, and ye People, hold right on !
Your task not yet is done :
Pursue the blow, . . ye know your foe, . .
Complete the happy work so well begun.
Hold on, and be your aim with all your strength
Loudly proclaim'd and steadily pursued ;
So shall this fatal Tyranny at length
Before the arms of Freedom fall subdued.
Then, when the waters of the flood abate,
The Dove her resting-place secure may find :
And France restored, and shaking off her chain,
Shall join the Avengers in the joyful strain,
Glory to God ! Deliverance for Mankind !

NOTES.

NOTES.

That no weak heart, no abject mind possessed
Her counsels. IV.

" Can any man of sense," said the Edinburgh Review, " does
any plain, unaffected man, above the level of a drivelling
courtier or a feeble fanatic, dare to say he can look at this
impending contest, without trembling every inch of him, for
the result ? "—*No. XXIV.* p. 441.

With all proper deference to so eminent a critic, I would
venture to observe, that trembling has been usually supposed
to be a symptom of feebleness, and that the case in point has
certainly not belied the received opinion.

Onoro's Springs. V.

Fuentes d'Onoro. This name has sometimes been rendered
Fountains of Honour, by an easy mistake, or a pardonable
licence.

Bear witness, those Old Towers. VI.

Torres Vedras. *Turres Veteres,* . . a name so old as to have
been given when the Latin tongue was the language of
Portugal. This town is said to have been founded by the
Turduli, a short time before the commencement of the Christian Æra.

In remembering the lines of Torres Vedras, the opinion of
the wise men of the North ought not to be forgotten, " If they

(the French) do not make an effort to drive us out of Portugal, it is because we are better there than any where else. We fear they will not leave us on the Tagus many days longer than suits their own purposes." — *Edinburgh Rev. No. XXVII.* p. 263.

The opinion is delivered with happy precision of language: . . Our troops were indeed, to use the same neat and felicitous expression, ' *better there than any where else.*'

> *And thou, Busaco, on whose sacred height*
> *The astonish'd Carmelite,*
> *While those unwonted thunders shook his cell,*
> *Join'd with his prayers the fervour of the fight.*   VI.

Of Busaco, which is now as memorable in the military, as it has long been in the monastic history of Portugal, I have given an account in the second volume of Omniana.   Doña Bernarda Ferreira's poem upon this venerable place, contains much interesting and some beautiful description.   The first intelligence of the battle which reached England was in a letter written from this Convent by a Portugueze Commissary. " I have the happiness to acquaint you," said the writer, " that this night the French lost nine thousand men near the Convent of Busaco. . . I beg you not to consider this news as a fiction, . . for I, from where I am, saw them fall.   This place appears like the antechamber of Hell." . . What a contrast to the images which the following extracts present !

> Es pequeña aquella Iglesia,
>   Mas para pobres bastante ;
>   Pobre de todo adereço
>   Con que el rico suele ornarse.
> No ay alli plata, ni oro,
>   Telas y sedas no valen
>   Donde reyna la pobreza,
>   Que no para en bienes tales
> Asperando a los del Cielo

Los demas tiene por males,
Y rica de altos desseos
Menosprecia vanidades.
En el retablo se mira
El soberano estandarte,
Lecho donde con la Iglesia
Quiso Christo desposarse;
La tabla donde se salva
El misero naufragante
Del pielago de la culpa,
Y a puerto glorioso sale.
Con perfecion y concierto
Se adereçan los altares
(por manos de aquellos santos)
De bellas flores suaves.
En toscos vasos de corcho
Lustran texidos con arte
Los variados ramilletes
Mas que en el oro el esmalte.
La florida rama verde
Que en aquellos bosques nace,
Da colgaduras al templo,
Y los brocados abate.
En dias de mayor fiesta
Esto con excessos hazen,
Y al suelo por alcatifas
Diversas flores reparten.
Huele el divino aposento,
Hurtando sutil el ayre
A las rosas y boninas
Mil olores que derrame.
Humildes estan las celdas
De aquellos humildes padres,
Cercando al sacro edificio
Do tienen su caro amante.
Cada celda muy pequeña
Encierra pobreza grande,

o 2

Que en competencia sus dueños
Gustan de mortificarse.
Despues que alli entro el silencio,
No quiso que mas sonasse
Ruydo que aquel que forma
Entre los ramos el ayre;
El de las fuentes y arroyos,
Y de las parleras aves,
Porque si ellos por Dios lloran,
Ellas sus lagrimas canten.
De corcho tosco las puertas,
Tambien de pobreza imagen,
Son mas bellas en sus ojos
Que los Toscanos portales.
Es su cama estrecha tabla
Do apenas tendidos caben,
Porque hasta en ella durmiendo,
Crucificados descansen.
Una Cruz, y calavera
Que tienen siempre delante,
Con asperas disciplinas
Teñidas de propria sangre,
Son alhajas de su casa;
Y en aquellas soledades
Hablando con sabios mudos
Suelen tal vez aliviarse;
Que a los hijos de Theresa
Tanto los libros aplacen,
Que en los yermos mas remotos
Les dan del dia una parte.
Tiene cada qual un huerto
(porque en el pueda ocuparse)
De arboles de espino, y flores
Siempre de olor liberales.
Libres ansi del tumulto
Que embaraça los mortales,
Ferverosas oraciones

Mandan a Dios cada instante.
Sus devotos exercicios
    No se los perturba nadie;
    Ni sus penitencias hallan
    Testigos que las estrañen.
Qual con cadenas de puas
    Tan duras como diamantes,
    Agudas y rigurosas
    Ciñe su afligida carne;
Qual con cilicios y sogas
    Asperrimas, intractables,
    De que jamas se les quitan
    Las cavernosas senales.

* * * * *

Aquel divino desierto
    Que Busaco denomina,
    Y es tambien denominado
    Del arbol de nuestra vida,
Se muestra sembrado a trechos
    De solitarias Ermitas,
    Que en espacios desiguales
    Unas de las otras distan.
Parece tocan las nubes,
    Para servirles de sillas,
    Las que coronando peñas
    Apenas toca la vista.
Yazen otras por los valles
    En las entrañas benignas
    De nuestra madre comun
    Que humilde se las inclina.
Qual en las concavidades
    De las rocas escondida,
    Que labro naturaleza
    Con perfecion infinita.
Qual entre las arboledas
    De verde rama vestida,

o 3

Informandoles de gracias
   Sus formas vegetativas.
Qual del cristalino arroyo
   Las bellas margenes pisa,
   Por lavar los pies descalços
   Entre sus candidas guijas,
Qual en el tronco del arbol
   Dentro en sus cortezas mismas,
   Por vencer en gracia al arte
   Naturaleza fabrica.
Unas aprieta con lazos
   Aquella planta lasciva
   Que hasta las piedras abraça
   Con ser tan duras y frias.
Otras de amarillos musgos
   Por el techo se matizan,
   Verdes, obscuros, y negros,
   Y de color de ceniza.
Toscos alli los portales
   De yerva y moho se pintan,
   Y de salitre se labran
   Que en gotas al agua imita.
Cada Ermitaño a la puerta
   Tiene una pequeña esquila,
   En el ramo de algun arbol
   Donde pendiente se arrima ;
O en el resquicio gracioso
   De alguna piedra metida,
   Y quando toca la Iglesia
   Todas a tocar se aplican.

Tagus and Zezere, in secret night,
  Ye saw the baffled ruffian take his flight ! VI.

Beacons of infamy they light the way,
  Where cowardice and cruelty unite,
To damn with double shame their ignominious flight.

O triumph for the Fiends of lust and wrath !
  Ne'er to be told, yet ne'er to be forgot,
What wanton horrors mark their wrackful path !
  The peasant butcher'd in his ruined cot,
The hoary priest even at the altar shot,
  Childhood and age given o'er to sword and flame,
Woman to infamy; no crime forgot,
  By which inventive demons might proclaim
Immortal hate to Man, and scorn of God's great name.

The rudest centinel, in Britain born,
  With horror paused to view the havoc done,
Gave his poor crust to feed some wretch forlorn,
  Wiped his stern eye, then fiercer grasp'd his gun.
               SCOTT's *Vision of Don Roderick.*

No cruelties recorded in history exceed those which were systematically committed by the French during their retreat from Portugal. " Their conduct, (says Lord Wellington in his dispatch of the 14th of March, 1811,) throughout this retreat, has been marked by a barbarity seldom equalled, and never surpassed.

" Even in the towns of Torres Novas, Thomar, and Pernes, in which the head-quarters of some of the corps had been for four months, and in which the inhabitants had been induced by promises of good treatment to remain, they were plundered and many of their houses destroyed on the night the enemy withdrew from their position; and they have since burnt every town and village through which they have passed. The Convent of Alcobaça was burnt by order from the French head-quarters. The Bishop's Palace, and the whole town of Leyria, in which General Drouet had had his head-quarters, shared the same fate; and there is not an inhabitant of the country, of any class or description, who has had any dealing or communication with the French army who has not had reason to repent of it, or to complain of them. This is the mode in which the promises have been performed, and the assurances have been fulfilled, which were held out in the proclamation of the French commander in chief, in which he told the inhabitants of Portugal, that he was not come to make war upon them, but with a powerful army of one hundred and ten thousand men to drive the English into the sea. It is to be hoped, that the example of what has occurred in this country will teach the people of this and other nations what value they ought to place on such promises and assurances, and that there is no security for life or for any thing that renders life valuable, except in decided resistance to the enemy."

As exact an account of these atrocities was collected as it was possible to obtain, . . and that record will for ever make the French name detested in Portugal. In the single diocese of Coimbra, 2969 persons, men, women, and children, were murdered, . . every one with some shocking circumstance of aggravated cruelty. . . *Nem huma só das* 2969 *mortes commettidas pelo inimigo, deixou de ser atroz e dolorosissima.* (Breve Memoria dos Estragos Causados no Bispado de Coimbra pelo Exercito Francez, commandado pelo General Massena. Extrahida das Enformaçoens que deram os Reverendos Parocos, e remettida a Junta dos Socorros da Subscripsam Britannica, pelo Reverendo Provisor Governador do mesmo Bispado, p. 12.) Some details are given in this brief Memorial. *A de tel forfaits,* says J. J. Rousseau, *celui qui detourne ses regards est un lâche, un deserteur de la justice : la veritable humanité les envisage pour les connoitre, pour les juger, pour les detester.* (Le Levite d'Ephraim.) I will not, however, in this place repeat abominations which at once outrage humanity and disgrace human nature.

When the French, in 1792, entered Spire, some of them began to commit excesses which would soon have led to a general sack. Custine immediately ordered a captain, two officers, and a whole company to be shot. This dreadful example, he told the National Convention, he considered as the only means of saving the honour of the French Nation, . . and it met with the approbation of the whole army. But the French armies had not then been systematically brutalized.

It was reserved for Buonaparte to render them infamous, as well as to lead them to destruction.

The French soldier, says Capmany, is executioner and robber at the same time : he leaves the unhappy wretch who is delivered over to his mercy, naked to the skin, . . stripping off the clothes that they may not be torn by the musket-shot ! . . The pen falls from my hand, and I cannot proceed !

Para que se junte a esta crueldad la mayor infamia, el soldado Frances es verdugo y ladron en una pieza ; dexa en cueros vivos al malaventurado que entregan a su discrecion, quitandole la ropa antes que los fusilazos se la destrozen. La pluma se cae de la mano, y no puede proseguir. — Centinela, contra Franceses, P. 2. p. 35.

Yet the Edinburgh Review says, " the hatred of the name of a Frenchman in Spain has been such as the reality will by no means justify ; and the detestation of the French government has, among the inferior orders, been carried to a pitch wholly unauthorized by its proceedings towards them." *No. XXVII.* p. 262. This passage might be read with astonishment, if any thing absurd, any thing mischievous, or any thing false, could excite surprise when it comes from that quarter.

> *What though the Tyrant, drunk with power,*
> *Might vaunt himself, in impious hour,*
> *Lord and Disposer of this earthly ball ?* VII.

Lo he dicho varias veces, y lo repito ahora, que las tres epocas terribles en los annales del mundo son, el diluvio universal, Mahoma, y Buonaparte. Aque pretendia convertir todas las religiones en una, y este todas las naciones, para ser el su cabeza. Aquel predicaba la unidad de Dios con la cimitarra ; y este no le nombra uno ni trino, pues solo predica, o hace predicar su propia divinidad, dexandose dar de sus infames y sacrilegos adoradores, los periodistas Franceses, el dictado de Todo-poderoso. El mismo se ha llegado a creer tal, y se ha hecho creer la cobardia y vileza de las naciones que se han dexado subyugar. Solo la España le ha obligado a reconnocerse, que no era antes, ni es ahora, sino un

hombre, y hombre muy pequeño, a quien la fortuna ciega ha
hecho grande a los ojos de los pueblos espantados del terror de su
nombre, que miden la grandeza del poder por la de las atro-
cidades.—Centinela, contra Franceses, p. 48.

" I have sometimes said, and I repeat it now, that the three
terrible epochs in the annals of the World are the General
Deluge, Mahommed, and Buonaparte.   Mahommed pre-
tended to convert all religions into one, and this man all nations
into one, in order to make himself their head.   Mahommed
preached the unity of God with the scimitar; and this man
neither his Unity nor his Trinity, for he neither preaches,
nor causes to be preached, any thing except his own Divinity,
letting his infamous and sacrilegious adorers, the French
journalists, give him the appellation of Almighty.   He has
gone so far as to believe himself such, and the cowardice and
baseness of the nations who have suffered themselves to be
subdued, have made him believe it. Spain alone has compelled
him to know himself, that he neither was formerly nor is now
any thing more than a mere man, and a very little one, whom
blind Fortune has made appear great in the eyes of people
astonished at the terror of his name, and measuring the greatness of his power by that of his atrocities."

> *Knowing that nought could e'er appal*
> *The Spaniard's fortitude.*   VII.

" The fate of Spain, we think, *is decided,* and that fine and
misguided country has probably yielded, by this time, to the
fate which has fallen on the greater part of continental Europe.
Her European dominions have yielded already to the unrelaxing
grasp of the insatiable conqueror." — Edinburgh Review,
No. XXVI. p. 298.

" The fundamental position which we ventured to lay down
respecting the Spanish question was this: . . that the spirit of
the people, however enthusiastic and universal, was in its
nature more uncertain and short-lived, more likely to be ex-
tinguished by reverses, or to go out of itself amidst the delays

of a protracted contest, than the steady, regular, moderate feeling which calls out disciplined troops, and marshals them under known leaders, and supplies them by systematic arrangements : . . a proposition so plain and obvious, that if it escaped ridicule as a truism, it might have been reasonably expected to avoid the penalties of heresy and paradox. *The event has indeed woefully proved its truth."* — Edinburgh Rev. No. XXVII. p. 246.

These gentlemen could see no principle of permanence in the character of the Spaniards, and no proof of it in their history ; . . and they could discover no principle of dissolution in the system of Buonaparte ; . . a system founded upon force and falsehood, in direct opposition to the interest of his own subjects and to the feelings of human nature.

The Campeador. VIII.

The Cid, Rodrigo Diaz de Bivar. The word has been variously explained, but its origin seems to be satisfactorily traced by Verstegan in his explanation of some of our English surnames.

" Cemp or Kemp, properly one that fighteth hand to hand, whereunto the name in Teutonic of Kemp-fight accordeth, and in French of Combat.

" Certain among the ancient Germans made profession of being Camp-fighters or Kemp-fighters, for all is one ; and among the Danes and Swedes were the like, as Scarcater, Arngrim, Arnerod, Haldan, and sundry others. They were also called Kempanas, whereof is derived our name of Campion, which after the French orthography some pronounce Champion."

" Dene or Den is the termination of sundry of our surnames, as for example of Camden, which I take anciently to have been Campden, and signifieth the Dene or Dale belonging to some Cemp or Camp-fighter (for both is one) in our now used language called a Champion, but in the Teutonic a Campion. A Campden may also have been some place ap-

pointed for Campions, Combat-fighters, or men of arms to
encounter each other.   And so the place became afterward to
be the surname of him and his family that owned it, as others
in like sort have done."

" Kemp, .. of his profession of being a Kemper or Combat-
fighter, as divers in old time among our ancestors were."

Vengeance was the word.   X.

This feeling is forcibly expressed by Capmany.   *O Visperas
Sicilianas tan famosas en la historia, quando os podremos acom-
panar con completas, para que los Angeles canten laudes en el
cielo.* — Centinela, contra Fraceses, p. 96.

O Sicilian Vespers! so famous in history, when shall we be
able to accompany you with Complines, that the Angels may
sing Lauds in Heaven?

*Behold the awaken'd Moscovite
Meets the tyrant in his might.*   XVII.

Ecce iterum Crispinus!   What says the Edinburgh Review
concerning Russia?   " Considering how little that power has
shewn itself capable of effecting for the salvation of Europe, ..
how wretched the state of its subjects is under the present
government, .. how trifling an acquisition of strength the
common enemy could expect to obtain from the entire posses-
sion of its resources, we acknowledge that we should contemplate with great composure any change which might lay the
foundation of future improvement, and scatter the forces of
France over the dominion of the Czars."—*No. XXVIII.*
p. 460.

This is a choice passage.   The reasoning is worthy of the
writer's judgement, the feeling perfectly consistent with his
liberality, and the conclusion as consistent with his politics.

Up Germany ——
 —— *She rose as from the dead ;*
She broke her chains upon the oppressor's head.   XVI.

Hear the Edinburgh Reviewer!   " It would be as chimerical to expect a mutiny among the vassal states of France
who are the most impatient of her yoke, as amongst the inhabitants of Bourdeaux, or the conscripts of the years 1808
and 1809.   In making this comparison, we are indeed putting
the case much more strongly against France than the facts
warrant, for with the exception of Holland, and the States into
which the conscription has been introduced, either immediately,
or by means of large requisitions of men made to their Go-
vernments *, the changes effected by the French invasion have
been favourable to the individual happiness of the inhabitants †,
so that the hatred of France is liable to considerable diminu-
tion, inasmuch as the national antipathy and spirit of independence are gradually undermined by the solid benefits which
the change of masters has conferred."—*No. XXVIII.* p. 458.

Great as a statesman, profound as a philosopher, amiable as
an optimist of the Pangloss school,.. but not altogether fortu-
nate as a Prophet!

* N.B. These little exceptions include all the countries which were an-
nexed to the French Empire, all Italy, and all the States of the Confedera-
tion of the Rhine.
† Particularly the commercial part of them.

POSTSCRIPT.

1821.

As a proper accompaniment to the preceding Notes, upon their republication, I subjoin an extract from a *William- Smithic* epistle, begun a few years ago upon sufficient provocation, but left unfinished, because better employments delayed its completion till the offence, gross as is was, seemed no longer deserving of a thought.

*   *   *   *   *

My fortune has been somewhat remarkable in this respect, that, bestowing less attention than most men upon contemporary literature, I am supposed to concern myself with it in a degree which would leave me no time for any worthier occupation.   Half the persons who are wounded in the Quarterly Review fix upon me as the object of their resentment; some, because they are conscious of having deserved chastisement at my hands ; others, because they give credit to an empty report, a lying assertion, or their own conceited sagacity in discovering a writer by his style.   As for the former, they flatter themselves egregiously in supposing that I should throw away my anger upon such subjects.   But by the latter I would willingly have it understood, that I heartily disapprove the present fashion of criticism, and sincerely wish that you, Sir, and your friend, had taken out an exclusive patent for it, when you brought it into vogue.

With regard to literary assailants, I should as little think of resenting their attacks in anger, as of making war upon midges and mosquitos.   I have therefore never noticed your amiable colleague in his critical capacity.   Let him blunder and misquote, and misrepresent, and contradict himself in the same page, or in the same sentence, with as much ingenuity as he will : " 'T is his vocation, Hal !" and some allowances must be made for habit.   I remember what Lord Anson's linguist said to him at Canton, upon the detection of some notable act of dishonesty : *Chinaman very great rogue truly : but hab fashion : no can help.*" Concerning *me*, and any composition of mine, it is impossible that this gentleman can write wisely unless his nature should undergo a radical change, for it is written in the wisest book which ever proceeded from mere humanity, that " into a malicious soul, wisdom shall not enter."

You may have seen a mastiff of the right English breed assailed by a little, impertinent, noisy, meddling cur, who runs behind him, snapping and barking at his heels, and sometimes gets staggered by a chance-whisk of his tail. The mastiff continues his way peaceably; or if he condescends to notice the yelper, it is only by stopping half a minute, and lifting his leg over him. Just such, Sir, is the notice which I bestow upon your colleague in his critical character.

But for F. J. *Philomath. and Professor of the Occult Sciences,* he is a grave personage, whose political and prophetical pretensions entitle him to high consideration in these days. He is as great a man as Lilly in the time of the Commonwealth, or as Partridge after him. It is well known what infinite pains he bestowed in casting the nativities of Lord Wellington, Buonaparte, and the Emperor of Russia, . . all for the good of mankind! and it is also notorious that he mistook the aspects, and made some very unfortunate errors in his predictions. At a time when he was considerably indisposed in consequence of this mortification, I took the liberty of administering to him a dose of his own words, mixed, perhaps, Sir, with a few of yours, for you were his fellow-student in astrology, and are known to have assisted him in these his calculations. The medicine was given in the form of extract; but the patient could not have used more wry faces had it been extract of coloquintida. And indeed it produced a most unpleasant effect. Ever since that time his paroxysms have been more violent, and he has been troubled with occasional ravings, accompanied with periodical discharges of bile in its most offensive state. Nevertheless, dreadfully bilious as he is, and tormented with acrid humours, it is hoped that by a cool diet, by the proper use of refrigerants, above all, by paying due at-

tention to the state of the *primæ viæ*, and observing a strict
abstinence from the Quarterly Review, the danger of a *cholera
morbus* may be averted.

I have not been travelling out of the record while thus inci-
dentally noticing a personage with whom you, Sir, are more
naturally and properly associated than I have been with Mr.
Wordsworth, this your colleague and you being the Gog and
Magog of the Edinburgh Review. Had it not been for a
difference of opinion upon political points between myself
and certain writers in that journal who laid claim to the
faculty of the second sight, I suspect that I should never have
incurred your hostility. What those points of difference were
I must here be permitted to set forth for the satisfaction of
those readers who may not be so well acquainted with them
as you are: they related to the possibility of carrying on the
late war to an honourable and successful termination.

It was in our state of feeling, Sir, as well as in our state of
knowledge that we differed, in our desires as much as in our
judgement. They predicted for us nothing but disgrace and
defeat: *predicted* is the word; for they themselves assured
us that they were " *seriously occupied with the destinies of
Europe and of mankind ;* "—

" As who should say I am Sir Oracle! "

They ridiculed " *the romantic hopes of the English nation,*" and
imputed the spirit by which the glory of that nation has been
raised to its highest point, and the deliverance of Europe
accomplished, to " *the tricks of a paltry and interested party.*"
They said that events had " *verified their predictions,*" had
" *more than justified their worst forebodings.*" They told us in
1810 that the fate of Spain was *decided,* and that that " *misguided*" country (misguided in having ventured to resist the
most insolent usurpation that ever was attempted) " *had yielded
to the Conqueror.*" This manner of speaking of an event in the
preter-pluperfect tense, before it has come to pass, may be
either a slight grammatical slip, or a prophetical figure of

speech : but, as old Dr. Eachard says, " I hate all small am-
biguous surmises, all quivering and mincing conjectures : give
me the lusty and bold thinker, who when he undertakes to
prophesy does it punctually." " *It would be blood-thirsty and
cruel,*" they said, " *to foment petty insurrections,* (meaning the
war in Spain and Portugal,) *after the only contest is over from
which any good can spring in the present unfortunate state of
affairs.*" " *France has conquered Europe. This is the melancholy truth. Shut our eyes to it as we may, there can be no
doubt about the matter. For the present, peace and submission
must be the lot of the vanquished.*" " *Let us hear no more of
objections to a Buonaparte ruling in Spain.*"

" Harry, the wish was father to that thought ! "

They told us that if Lord Wellington was not driven out of
Portugal, it was because the French government thought him
" *better there than any where else.*" They told us they were
prepared to " *contemplate with great composure*" the conquest of
Russia, by Buonaparte, as a " change which would lay the
foundation of future improvement in the dominions of the
Czars." —

" Si mens sit læta tibi crederis esse propheta,

says an old Leonine rhymester. — And as for expecting " *a*
MUTINY (hear Germany ! for so they qualified it !) *amongst the
vassal states of France, it would be as chimerical,*" they said, " *as
to expect one amongst the inhabitants of Bourdeaux.*" And here
these lucky prophets were peculiarly felicitous ; the inhabitants
of Bourdeaux having been the first people in France who threw
off the yoke of Buonaparte's tyranny, and mounted the white
cockade.

" Omnia jam fiunt, fieri quæ posse negabam ."

Poor Oracle ! the face is double-bronzed ; and yet it is but
a wooden head !

VOL. III. P

I stood upon firm ground, while they were sticking in the Slough of Despond. *Hinc illæ lacrymæ!* I charged them at the time with ignorance, presumption, and pusillanimity. And now, Sir, I ask of you, were they or were they not ignorant? Here are their assertions! — Were they or were they not presumptuous? Here are their predictions! — Were they or were they not pusillanimous? Have they or have they not been confuted, and confounded, and exposed, and shamed, and stultified, by the event?

They who know me will bear witness, that, before a rumour of war was heard from the Peninsula, I had looked toward that quarter as the point where we might hope first to see the horizon open; and that, from the hour in which the struggle commenced, I never doubted of its final success, provided England should do its duty : this confidence was founded upon a knowledge of the country and the people, and upon the principles which were then and there first brought into action against the enemy. At the time when every effort was made (as you, Sir, well know) to vilify and disgust our allies, to discourage the public, to impede the measures of government, to derange its finances, and thereby cut off its means, to paralyse the arm and deaden the heart of England; — when we were told of the irresistible power and perfect policy of Buonaparte, the consummate skill of his generals, and the invincibility of his armies, my language was this : " The one business of England is to abate the power of France : that power she must beat down, or fall herself; that power she will beat down, if she do but strenuously put forth her own mighty means." And again, — " For our soldiers to equal our seamen, it is only necessary for them to be equally well commanded. They have the same heart and soul, as well as the same flesh and blood. Too much, indeed, may be exacted from them in a retreat: but set their face toward a foe, and there is nothing within the reach of human achievement which they cannot perform." And again ; — " Carry on the war with all the heart, and with all the soul, and with all the strength, of this mighty empire, and you will beat down the power of France."

Was I wrong, Sir? Or has the event corresponded to this confidence?

Αμέραι επιλοιποι
ιάρτυρες σοφώτατοι.

Bear witness Torres Vedras, Salamanca, and Vittoria ! Bear witness Orthies and Thoulouse ! Bear witness Waterloo, and that miserable tyrant, who was then making and unmaking kings with a breath, and now frets upon the rock of St. Helena, like a tiger in his cage !

* * * * * *

ODES.

ODE,

WRITTEN DURING THE NEGOCIATIONS WITH
BUONAPARTE, IN JANUARY, 1814.

1.

WHO counsels peace at this momentous hour,
When God hath given deliverance to the oppress'd,
And to the injured power?
Who counsels peace, when Vengeance like a flood
Rolls on, no longer now to be repress'd;
When innocent blood
From the four corners of the world cries out
For justice upon one accursed head;
When Freedom hath her holy banners spread
Over all nations, now in one just cause
United; when with one sublime accord
Europe throws off the yoke abhorr'd,
And Loyalty and Faith and Ancient Laws
Follow the avenging sword!

2.

Woe, woe to England! woe and endless shame,
If this heroic land,
False to her feelings and unspotted fame,
Hold out the olive to the Tyrant's hand!
Woe to the world, if Buonaparte's throne
Be suffer'd still to stand!
For by what names shall Right and Wrong be known,..

P 4

What new and courtly phrases must we feign
For Falsehood, Murder, and all monstrous crimes,
If that perfidious Corsican maintain
Still his detested reign,
And France, who yearns even now to break her chain,
Beneath his iron rule be left to groan?
No! by the innumerable dead,
Whose blood hath for his lust of power been shed,
Death only can for his foul deeds atone;
That peace which Death and Judgement can bestow,
That peace be Buonaparte's, .. that alone!

3.

For sooner shall the Ethiop change his skin,
Or from the Leopard shall her spots depart,
Than this man change his old flagitious heart.
Have ye not seen him in the balance weigh'd,
And there found wanting? On the stage of blood
Foremost the resolute adventurer stood;
And when, by many a battle won,
He placed upon his brow the crown,
Curbing delirious France beneath his sway,
Then, like Octavius in old time,
Fair name might he have handed down,
Effacing many a stain of former crime.
Fool! should he cast away that bright renown!
Fool! the redemption proffer'd should he lose!
When Heaven such grace vouchsafed him that the way
To Good and Evil lay
Before him, which to choose.

4.

But Evil was his Good,
For all too long in blood had he been nurst,
And ne'er was earth with verier tyrant curst.
Bold man and bad,
Remorseless, godless, full of fraud and lies,
And black with murders and with perjuries,
Himself in Hell's whole panoply he clad ;
No law but his own headstrong will he knew,
No counsellor but his own wicked heart.
From evil thus portentous strength he drew,
And trampled under foot all human ties,
All holy laws, all natural charities.

5.

O France ! beneath this fierce Barbarian's sway
Disgraced thou art to all succeeding times ;
Rapine, and blood, and fire have mark'd thy way,
All loathsome, all unutterable crimes.
A curse is on thee, France ! from far and wide
It hath gone up to Heaven. All lands have cried
For vengeance upon thy detested head !
All nations curse thee, France ! for wheresoe'er
In peace or war thy banner hath been spread,
All forms of human woe have follow'd there.
The Living and the Dead
Cry out alike against thee ! They who bear,
Crouching beneath its weight, thine iron yoke,
Join in the bitterness of secret prayer
The voice of that innumerable throng,
Whose slaughter'd spirits day and night invoke
The Everlasting Judge of right and wrong,
How long, O Lord ! Holy and Just, how long !

6.

A merciless oppressor hast thou been,
  Thyself remorselessly oppress'd meantime;
Greedy of war, when all that thou couldst gain
  Was but to dye thy soul with deeper crime,
    And rivet faster round thyself the chain.
  O blind to honour, and to interest blind,
    When thus in abject servitude resign'd
To this barbarian upstart, thou couldst brave
  God's justice, and the heart of human kind!
Madly thou thoughtest to enslave the world,
    Thyself the while a miserable slave.
  Behold the flag of vengeance is unfurl'd!
The dreadful armies of the North advance;
While England, Portugal, and Spain combined,
  Give their triumphant banners to the wind,
  And stand victorious in the fields of France.

7.

One man hath been for ten long wretched years
The cause of all this blood and all these tears;
  One man in this most aweful point of time
  Draws on thy danger, as he caused thy crime.
    Wait not too long the event,
  For now whole Europe comes against thee bent,
His wiles and their own strength the nations know
  Wise from past wrongs, on future peace intent,
    The People and the Princes, with one mind,
  From all parts move against the general foe:
    One act of justice, one atoning blow,
      One execrable head laid low,
  Even yet, O France! averts thy punishment.

Open thine eyes ! too long hast thou been blind;
Take vengeance for thyself, and for mankind !

8.

France ! if thou lovest thine ancient fame,
Revenge thy sufferings and thy shame !
By the bones which bleach on Jaffa's beach ;
By the blood which on Domingo's shore
Hath clogg'd the carrion-birds with gore ;
By the flesh which gorged the wolves of Spain,
Or stiffen'd on the snowy plain
Of frozen Moscovy ;
By the bodies which lie all open to the sky,
Tracking from Elbe to Rhine the Tyrant's flight ;
By the widow's and the orphan's cry ;
By the childless parent's misery ;
By the lives which he hath shed ;
By the ruin he hath spread ;
By the prayers which rise for curses on his head ;
Redeem, O France ! thine ancient fame,
Revenge thy sufferings and thy shame,
Open thine eyes !.. too long hast thou been blind;
Take vengeance for thyself, and for mankind !

9.

By those horrors which the night
Witness'd, when the torches' light
To the assembled murderers show'd
Where the blood of Condé flow'd ;
By thy murder'd Pichegru's fame ;
By murder'd Wright,.. an English name ;

By murder'd Palm's atrocious doom;
    By murder'd Hofer's martyrdom;
Oh! by the virtuous blood thus vilely spilt,
    The Villain's own peculiar private guilt,
·Open thine eyes! too long hast thou been blind!
    Take vengeance for thyself and for mankind!

Keswick.

ODE,

WRITTEN DURING THE WAR WITH AMERICA,
1814.

1.

WHEN shall the Island Queen of Ocean lay
The thunderbolt aside,
And, twining olives with her laurel crown,
Rest in the Bower of Peace ?

2.

Not long may this unnatural strife endure
Beyond the Atlantic deep ;
Not long may men, with vain ambition drunk,
And insolent in wrong,
Afflict with their misrule the indignant land
Where Washington hath left
His aweful memory
A light for after times !
Vile instruments of fallen Tyranny,
In their own annals, by their countrymen,
For lasting shame shall they be written down.
Soon may the better Genius there prevail !
Then will the Island Queen of Ocean lay
The thunderbolt aside,
And, twining olives with her laurel crown,
Rest in the Bower of Peace.

3.

But not in ignominious ease,
Within the Bower of Peace supine,
The Ocean Queen shall rest !
Her other toils await, . .
A holier warfare, . . nobler victories ;
And amaranthine wreaths,
Which, when the laurel crown grows sere,
Will live for ever green.

4.

Hear me, O England ! rightly may I claim
Thy favourable audience, Queen of Isles,
My Mother-land revered !
For in the perilous hour,
When weaker spirits stood aghast,
And reptile tongues, to thy dishonour bold,
Spit their dull venom on the public ear,
My voice was heard, . . a voice of hope,
Of confidence and joy, . . .
Yea of such prophecy
As Wisdom to her sons doth aye vouchsafe,
When with pure heart and diligent desire
They seek the fountain springs,
And of the Ages past
Take counsel reverently.

5.

Nobly hast thou stood up
Against the foulest Tyranny that ere,
In elder or in later times,
Hath outraged human kind.

ᐧO glorious England! thou hast borne thyself
Religiously and bravely in that strife ;
And happier victory hath blest thine arms
Than, in the days of yore,
Thine own Plantagenets achieved,
Or Marlborough, wise in council as in field,
Or Wolfe, heroic name
Now gird thyself for other war ;
Look round thee, and behold what ills,
Remediable and yet unremedied,
Afflict man's wretched race !
Put on the panoply of faith !
Bestir thyself against thine inward foes,
Ignorance and Want, with all their brood
Of miseries and of crimes.

6.

Powerful thou art : imperial Rome,
When in the Augustan age she closed
The temple of the two-faced God,
Could boast no power like thine.
Less opulent was Spain,
When Mexico her sumless riches sent
To that proud monarchy ;
And Hayti's ransack'd caverns gave their gold ;
And from Potosi's recent veins
The unabating stream of treasure flow'd.
And blest art thou, above all nations blest,
For thou art Freedom's own beloved Isle !
The light of Science shines
Conspicuous like a beacon on thy shores ;
Thy martyrs purchased at the stake

Faith uncorrupt for thine inheritance ;
And by thine hearths Domestic Purity,
Safe from the infection of a tainted age,
Hath kept her sanctuaries.
Yet, O dear England! powerful as thou art,
And rich and wise and blest,
Yet would I see thee, O my Mother-land!
Mightier and wealthier, wiser, happier still!

7.

For still doth Ignorance
Maintain large empire here,
Dark and unblest amid surrounding light ;
Even as within this favour'd spot,
Earth's wonder and her pride,
The traveller on his way
Beholds with weary eye
Bleak moorland, noxious fen, and lonely heath,
In drear extension spread.
Oh grief! that spirits of celestial seed,
Whom ever-teeming Nature hath brought forth
With all the human faculties divine
Of sense and soul endued, ..
Disherited of knowledge and of bliss,
Mere creatures of brute life,
Should grope in darkness lost !

8.

Must this reproach endure ?
Honour and praise to him
The universal friend,
The general benefactor of mankind ;

He who from Coromandel's shores
His perfected discovery brought ;
He by whose generous toils
This foul reproach ere long shall be effaced,
This root of evil be eradicate !
Yea, generations yet unborn
Shall owe their weal to him,
And future nations bless
The honour'd name of Bell.

9.

Now may that blessed edifice
Of public good be rear'd
Which holy Edward traced,
The spotless Tudor, he whom Death
Too early summon'd to his heavenly throne.
For Brunswick's line was this great work reserved,
For Brunswick's fated line ;
They who from papal darkness, and the thrall
Of that worst bondage which doth hold
The immortal spirit chain'd,
Saved us in happy hour.
Fitly for them was this great work reserved ;
So, Britain, shall thine aged monarch's wish
Receive its due accomplishment,
That wish which with the good,
(Had he no other praise,)
Through all succeeding times would rank his name,
That all within his realms
Might learn the Book, which all
Who rightly learn shall live.

10.

From public fountains the perennial stream
Of public weal must flow.
O England ! wheresoe'er thy churches stand,
There on that sacred ground,
Where the rich harvest of mortality
Is laid, as in a garner, treasured up,
There plant the Tree of Knowledge ! Water it
With thy perpetual bounty ! It shall spread
Its branches o'er the venerable pile,
Shield it against the storm,
And bring forth fruits of life.

11.

Train up thy children, England ! in the ways.
Of righteousness, and feed them with the bread
Of wholesome doctrine. Where hast thou thy mines
But in their industry ?
Thy bulwarks where, but in their breasts ?
Thy might, but in their arms ?
Shall not their numbers therefore be thy wealth,
Thy strength, thy power, thy safety, and thy pride ?
Oh grief then, grief and shame,
If, in this flourishing land,
There should be dwellings where the new-born babe
Doth bring unto its parent's soul no joy !
Where squalid Poverty
Receives it at its birth,
And on her wither'd knees
Gives it the scanty food of discontent !

12.

Queen of the Seas! enlarge thyself;
Redundant as thou art of life and power,
Be thou the hive of nations,
And send thy swarms abroad!
Send them like Greece of old,
With arts and science to enrich
The uncultivated earth;
But with more precious gifts than Greece or Tyre
Or elder Egypt, to the world bequeath'd;
Just laws, and rightful polity,
And, crowning all, the dearest boon of Heaven,
Its word and will reveal'd.
Queen of the Seas! enlarge
The place of thy pavilion.   Let them stretch
The curtains of thine habitations forth;
Spare not; but lengthen thou
Thy cords, make strong thy stakes.

13.

Queen of the Seas! enlarge thyself;
Send thou thy swarms abroad!
For in the years to come,
Though centuries or millenniums intervene,
Where'er thy progeny,
Thy language, and thy spirit shall be found, ..
If on Ontario's shores,
Or late-explored Missouri's pastures wide,
Or in that Austral world long sought,
The many-isled Pacific, .. yea where waves,
Now breaking over coral reefs, affright
The venturous mariner,

When islands shall have grown, and cities risen
In cocoa groves embower'd ; ..
Where'er thy language lives,
By whatsoever name the land be call'd,
That land is English still, and there
Thy influential spirit dwells and reigns.
Thrones fall, and Dynasties are changed ;
Empires decay and sink
Beneath their own unwieldy weight ;
Dominion passeth like a cloud away :
The imperishable mind
Survives all meaner things.

14.

Train up thy children, England, in the ways
Of righteousness, and feed them with the bread
Of wholesome doctrine.   Send thy swarms abroad !
Send forth thy humanizing arts,
Thy stirring enterprize,
Thy liberal polity, thy Gospel light !
Illume the dark idolater,
Reclaim the savage !   O thou Ocean Queen !
Be these thy toils when thou hast laid
The thunderbolt aside :
He who hath blest thine arms
Will bless thee in these holy works of Peace !
Father ! thy kingdom come, and as in Heaven
Thy will be done on Earth !

Keswick.

CARMINA AULICA,

WRITTEN IN 1814,

ON

THE ARRIVAL OF THE ALLIED SOVEREIGNS
IN ENGLAND.

'Εχω καλά τε φράσαι, τόλμα τέ μοι
Εὐθεῖα γλῶσσαν ὀρνύει λέγειν.
PINDAR, OLYMP. XIII.

ODE

TO HIS ROYAL HIGHNESS THE PRINCE REGENT
OF THE UNITED KINGDOM OF GREAT BRITAIN
AND IRELAND.

1.

PRINCE of the mighty Isle!
Proud day for thee and for thy kingdoms this,
When Britain round her spear
The olive garland twines, by Victory won.

2.

Rightly may'st thou rejoice,
For in a day of darkness and of storms,
An evil day, a day of woe,
To thee the sceptre fell.
The Continent was leagued,
It's numbers wielded by one will,
Against the mighty Isle;
All shores were hostile to the Red Cross flag,
All ports against it closed ;
Save where, behind their ramparts driven,
The Spaniard, and the faithful Portugal,
Each on the utmost limits of his land,
Invincible of heart,
Stood firm, and put their trust
In their good cause and thee.

Q 4

3.

Such perils menaced from abroad ;
At home worse dangers compass'd thee,
Where shallow counsellors,
A weak but clamorous crew,
Pester'd the land, and with their withering breath
Poison'd the public ear.
For peace the feeble raised their factious cry :
Oh, madness, to resist
The Invincible in arms !
Seek the peace-garland from his dreadful hand !
And at the Tyrant's feet
They would have knelt to take
The wreath of aconite for Britain's brow.
Prince of the mighty Isle !
Rightly may'st thou rejoice,
For in the day of danger thou did'st turn
From their vile counsels thine indignant heart ;
Rightly may'st thou rejoice,
When Britain round her spear
The olive-garland twines, by Victory won.

4.

Rejoice, thou mighty Isle,
Queen of the Seas! rejoice ;
Ring round, ye merry bells,
Till every steeple rock,
And the wide air grow giddy with your joy !
Flow streamers to the breeze !
And ye victorious banners to the sun
Unroll the proud Red Cross !
Now let the anvil rest ;

Shut up the loom, and open the school-doors,
   That young and old may with festivities
Hallow for memory, through all after years,
      This memorable time :
      This memorable time,
When Peace, long absent, long deplored, returns
Not as vile Faction would have brought her home
   Her countenance for shame abased,
      In servile weeds array'd,
      Submission leading her,
Fear, Sorrow, and Repentance following close;
   And War, scarce deigning to conceal
Beneath the mantle's folds his armed plight,
   Dogging her steps with deadly eye intent,
   Sure of his victim, and in devilish joy
      Laughing behind the mask.

5.

   Not thus doth Peace return ! . .
   A blessed visitant she comes, . . .
     Honour in his right hand
     Doth lead her like a bride ;
     And Victory goes before ;
Hope, Safety, and Prosperity, and Strength,
     Come in her joyful train.
     Now let the churches ring
     With high thanksgiving songs,
     And the full organ pour
     It's swelling peals to Heaven,
The while the grateful nation bless in prayer
Their Warriors and their Statesmen and their Prince,
   Whose will, whose mind, whose arm

Have thus with happy end their efforts crown'd.
Prince of the mighty Isle,
Rightly may'st thou rejoice,
When Britain round her spear
The olive-garland twines, by Victory won.

6.

Enjoy thy triumph now,
Prince of the mighty Isle!
Enjoy the rich reward, so rightly due,
When rescued nations, with one heart and voice,
Thy counsels bless and thee.
Thou on thine own Firm Island seest the while,
As if the tales of old Romance
Were but to typify these splendid days,
Princes and Potentates,
And Chiefs renown'd in arms,
From their great enterprize achieved,
In friendship and in joy collected here.

7.

Rejoice, thou mighty Isle!
Queen of the Seas ! rejoice ;
For ne'er in elder nor in later times
Have such illustrious guests
Honour'd thy silver shores.
No such assemblage shone in Edward's hall,
Nor brighter triumphs graced his glorious reign.
Prince of the mighty Isle,
Proud day for thee and for thy kingdoms this !
Rightly mayst thou rejoice,

When Britain round her spear
The olive-garland twines, by Victory won.

8.

Yet in the pomp of these festivities
One mournful thought will rise within thy mind,
The thought of Him who sits
In mental as in visual darkness lost.
How had his heart been fill'd
With deepest gratitude to Heaven,
Had he beheld this day !
O King of kings, and Lord of lords,
Thou who hast visited thus heavily
The anointed head, . .
Oh ! for one little interval,
One precious hour,
Remove the blindness from his soul,
That he may know it all,
And bless thee ere he die.

9.

Thou also should'st have seen
This harvest of thy hopes,
Thou whom the guilty act
Of a proud spirit overthrown,
Sent to thine early grave in evil hour !
Forget not him, my country, in thy joy ;
But let thy grateful hand
With laurel garlands hang
The tomb of Perceval.
Virtuous, and firm, and wise,
The Ark of Britain in her darkest day

He steer'd through stormy seas ;
And long shall Britain hold his memory dear,
And faithful History give
His meed of lasting praise.

10.

That earthly meed shall his compeers enjoy,
Britain's true counsellors,
Who see with just success their counsels crown'd.
They have their triumph now, to him denied;
Proud day for them is this !
Prince of the mighty Isle !
Proud day for them and thee,
When Britain round her spear
The olive-garland twines, by Victory won.

237

ODE

TO HIS IMPERIAL MAJESTY, ALEXANDER THE FIRST,
EMPEROR OF ALL THE RUSSIAS.

1.

CONQUEROR, Deliverer, Friend of human-kind!
The free, the happy, Island welcomes thee;
Thee from thy wasted realms,
So signally revenged;
From Prussia's rescued plains;
From Dresden's field of slaughter, where the ball,
Which struck Moreau's dear life,
Was turn'd from thy more precious head aside;
From Leipsic's dreadful day,
From Elbe, and Rhine, and Seine,
In thy career of conquest overpast;
From the proud Capital
Of haughty France subdued,
Then to her rightful line of Kings restored;
Thee, Alexander! thee, the Great, the Good,
The Glorious, the Beneficent, the Just,
Thee to her honour'd shores
The mighty Island welcomes in her joy.

2.

Sixscore full years have past,
Since to these friendly shores

Thy famous ancestor,
Illustrious PETER came.
Wise traveller he, who over Europe went,
Marking the ways of men ;
That so to his dear country, which then rose
Among the nations in uncultured strength,
He might bear back the stores
Of elder polity,
Its sciences and arts.
Little did then the industrious German think, . .
The soft Italian, lapt in luxury, . .
Helvetia's mountain sons, of freedom proud, . .
The patient Hollander,
Prosperous and warlike then, . .
Little thought they that in that farthest North,
From PETER's race should the Deliverer spring
Destined by Heaven to save
Art, Learning, Industry,
Beneath the bestial hoof of godless Might
All trampled in the dust.
As little did the French,
Vaunting the power of their Great Monarch then,
(His schemes of wide ambition yet uncheck'd,)
As little did they think,
That from rude Moscovy the stone should come,
To smite their huge Colossus, which bestrode
The subject Continent ;
And from its feet of clay,
Breaking the iron limbs and front of brass,
Strew the rejoicing Nations with the wreck.

3.

Roused as thou wert with insult and with wrong,
Who should have blamed thee if, in high-wrought mood
Of vengeance and the sense of injured power,
Thou from the flames which laid
The City of thy Fathers in the dust,
Had'st bid a spark be brought,
And borne it in thy tent,
Religiously by night and day preserved,
Till on Montmartre's height,
When open to thine arms,
Her last defence o'erthrown,
The guilty city lay,
Thou hadst call'd every Russian of thine host
To light his flambeau at the sacred flame,
And sent them through her streets,
And wrapt her roofs and towers,
Temples and palaces,
Her wealth and boasted spoils,
In one wide flood of fire,
Making the hated Nation feel herself
The miseries she had spread.

4.

Who should have blamed the Conqueror for that deed?
Yea, rather would not one exulting cry
Have risen from Elbe to Nile,
How is the Oppressor fallen !
Moscow's re-rising walls
Had rung with glad acclaim ;
Thanksgiving hymns had fill'd
Tyrol's rejoicing vales :

How is the Oppressor fallen !
The Germans in their grass-grown marts had met
To celebrate the deed ;
Holland's still waters had been starr'd
With festive lights, reflected there
From every house and hut,
From every town and tower ;
The Iberian and the Lusian's injured realms,
From all their mountain-holds,
From all their ravaged fields,
From cities sack'd, from violated fanes,
And from the sanctuary of every heart,
Had pour'd that pious strain,
How is the Oppressor fallen !
Righteous art thou, O Lord !
Thou Zaragoza, from thy sepulchres
Hadst join'd the hymn ; and from thine ashes thou,
Manresa, faithful still !
The blood that calls for vengeance in thy streets,
Madrid, and Porto thine,
And that which from the beach
Of Tarragona sent its cry to Heaven,
Had rested then appeased.
Orphans had clapt their hands,
And widows would have wept exulting tears,
And childless parents with a bitter joy
Have blest the avenging deed.

5.

But thou hadst seen enough
Of horrors, .. amply hadst avenged mankind.
Witness that dread retreat,

When God and nature smote
The Tyrant in his pride!
No wider ruin overtook
Sennacherib's impious host;
Nor when the frantic Persian led
His veterans to the Lybian sands;
Nor when united Greece
O'er the barbaric power that victory won
Which Europe yet may bless.
A fouler Tyrant cursed the groaning earth, ..
A fearfuller destruction was dispensed.
Victorious armies followed on his flight;
On every side he met
The Cossacks' dreadful spear;
On every side he saw
The injured nation rise,
Invincible in arms.
What myriads, victims of one wicked will,
Spent their last breath in curses on his head,
There where the soldiers' blood
Froze in the festering wound;
And nightly the cold moon
Saw sinking thousands in the snow lie down,
Whom there the morning found
Stiff, as their icy bed.

6.

Rear high the monument!
In Moscow and in proud Petropolis,
The brazen trophy build;
Cannon on cannon piled,
Till the huge column overtop your towers!

From France the Tyrant brought
These instruments of death
To work your overthrow ;
He left them in his flight
To form the eternal record of his own.
Raise, Russia, with thy spoils,
A nobler monument
Than e'er imperial Rome
Built in her plenitude of pride and power !
Still, Alexander ! on the banks of Seine,
Thy noblest monument
For future ages stands —
PARIS SUBDUED AND SPARED.

7.

Conqueror, Deliverer, Friend of human-kind,
The free, the happy Island welcomes thee !
Thee, Alexander ! thee, the Great, the Good,
The Glorious, the Beneficent, the Just !
Thee to her honour'd shores
The mighty Island welcomes in her joy.

ODE

1.

WELCOME to England, to the happy Isle,
Brave Prince of gallant people ! Welcome Thou,
In adverse as in prosperous fortunes tried,
Frederick, the well-beloved !
Greatest and best of that illustrious name,
Welcome to these free shores !
In glory art thou come,
Thy victory perfect, thy revenge complete.

2.

Enough of sorrow hast thou known,
Enough of evil hath thy realm endured,
Oppress'd but not debased,
When thine indignant soul,
Long suffering, bore its weight of heaviest woe.
But still, through that dark day
Unsullied honour was thy counsellor;
And Hope, that had its trust in Heaven,
And in the heart of man
Its strength, forsook thee not.
Thou had'st thy faithful people's love,
The sympathy of noble minds;
And wistfully, as one

R 2

Who through the weary night has long'd for day,
Looks eastward for the dawn,
So Germany to thee
Turn'd in her bondage her imploring eyes.

3.

Oh, grief of griefs, that Germany,
The wise, the virtuous land,
The land of mighty minds,
Should bend beneath the frothy Frenchman's yoke!
Oh, grief of griefs, to think
That she should groan in bonds,
She who had blest all nations with her gifts!
There had the light of Reformation risen,
The light of Knowledge there was burning clear.
Oh, grief, that her unhappy sons
Should toil and bleed and die,
To quench that sacred light,
The wretched agents of a tyrant's will!
How often hath their blood
In his accursed cause
Reek'd on the Spaniard's blade!
Their mangled bodies fed
The wolves and eagles of the Pyrenees;
Or stiffening in the snows of Moscovy,
Amid the ashes of the watch-fire lay,
Where dragging painfully their frozen limbs,
With life's last effort, in the flames they fell.

4.

Long, Frederick, did'st thou bear
Her sorrows and thine own;

Seven miserable years
In patience did'st thou feed thy heart with hope ;
Till, when the arm of God
Smote the blaspheming Tyrant in his pride,
And Alexander with the voice of power
Raised the glad cry, Deliverance for Mankind,
First of the Germans, Prussia broke her chains.

5.

Joy, joy for Germany,
For Europe, for the World,
When Prussia rose in arms !
Oh, what a spectacle
For present and for future times was there,
When for the public need
Wives gave their marriage rings,
And mothers, when their sons
The Band of Vengeance join'd,
Bade them return victorious from the field,
Or with their country fall.

6.

Twice o'er the field of death
The trembling scales of Fate hung equipoised :
For France, obsequious to her Tyrant still,
Mighty for evil, put forth all her power ;
And still beneath his hateful banners driven,
Against their father-land
Unwilling Germans bore unnatural arms.
What though the Boaster made his temples ring
With vain thanksgivings for each doubtful day, .
What though with false pretence of peace
His old insidious arts he tried, ..

R 3

The spell was broken! Austria threw her sword
Into the inclining scale,
And Leipsic saw the wrongs
Of Germany avenged.

7.

Ne'er till that aweful time had Europe seen
Such multitudes in arms;
Nor ever had the rising Sun beheld
Such mighty interests of mankind at stake;
Nor o'er so wide a scene
Of slaughter e'er had Night her curtain closed.
There, on the battle-field,
With one accord the grateful monarchs knelt,
And raised their voice to Heaven;
"The cause was thine, O Lord!
"O Lord! thy hand was here!"
What Conquerors e'er deserved
So proud, so pure a joy!
It was a moment when the exalted soul
Might almost wish to burst its mortal bounds,
Lest all of life to come
Vapid and void should seem
After that high-wrought hour.

8.

But thou hadst yet more toils,
More duties and more triumphs yet in store.
Elbe must not bound thine arms,
Nor on the banks of Rhine
Thine eagles check their flight;
When o'er that barrier stream,

Awakened Germany
Drove her invaders with such rout and wreck
As overtook the impious Gaul of old,
Laden with plunder, and from Delphi driven.

9.

Long had insulting France
Boasted her arms invincible,
Her soil inviolate;
At length the hour of retribution comes !
Avenging nations on all sides move on;
In Gascony the flag of England flies,
Triumphant, as of yore,
When sable Edward led his peerless host.
Behold the Spaniard and the Portugal,
For cities burnt, for violated fanes,
For murders, massacres,
All monstrous, all unutterable crimes,
Demanding vengeance with victorious cries,
Pour from the Pyrenees.
The Russian comes, his eye on Paris fix'd,
The flames of Moscow present to his heart;
The Austrian to efface
Ulm, Austerlitz, and Wagram's later shame;
Rejoicing Germany
With all her nations swells the avenging train;
And in the field and in the triumph first,
Thy banner, Frederick, floats.

10.

Six weeks in daily strife
The veteran Blucher bore the brunt of war.

Glorious old man,
The last and greatest of his master's school,
Long may he live to hear
The people bless his name !
Late be it ere the wreath
That crowns his silver hair
Adorn his monument !
Glorious old man,
How oft hath he discomfited
The boasted chiefs of France,
And foil'd her vaunting Tyrant's desperate rage !
Glorious old man,
Who from Silesia's fields,
O'er Elbe, and Rhine, and Seine,
From victory to victory marching on,
Made his heroic way ; till at the gates
Of Paris, open'd by his arms, he saw
His King triumphant stand.

11.

Bear back the sword of Frederick now !
The sword which France amid her spoils display'd,
Proud trophy of a day ignobly won.
With laurels wreathe the sword ;
Bear it in triumph back,
Thus gloriously regain'd ;
And when thou lay'st it in its honour'd place,
O Frederick, well-beloved,
Greatest and best of that illustrious name,
Lay by its side thine own,
A holier relic there !

12.

Frederick, the well beloved!
Welcome to these free shores,
To England welcome, to the happy Isle!
In glory art thou come,
Thy victory perfect, thy revenge complete.

O D E S.

ODE.

THE BATTLE OF ALGIERS.

1.

ONE day of dreadful occupation more,
Ere England's gallant ships
Shall, of their beauty, pomp, and power disrobed,
Like sea-birds on the sunny main,
Rock idly in the port.

2.

One day of dreadful occupation more !
A work of righteousness,
Yea, of sublimest mercy, must be done ;
England will break the oppressor's chain,
And set the captives free.

3.

Red cross of England, which all shores have seen
Triumphantly displayed,
Thou sacred banner of the glorious Isle,
Known wheresoever keel hath cut
The navigable deep ;

4.

Ne'er didst thou float more proudly o'er the storm
Of havoc and of death,
Than when, resisting fiercely, but in vain,
Algiers, her moony standard lowered,
And sign'd the conqueror's law.

5.

Oh, if the grave were sentient, as these Moors
In erring credence hold ;
And if the victims of captivity
Could in the silent tomb have heard
The thunder of the fight ;

6.

Sure their rejoicing dust upon that day
Had heaved the oppressive soil,
And earth been shaken like the mosques and towers,
When England on those guilty walls
Her fiery vengeance sent.

7.

Seldom hath victory given a joy like this, —
When the delivered slave
Revisits once again his own dear home,
And tells of all his sufferings past,
And blesses Exmouth's name.

8.

Far, far and wide along the Italian shores,
That holy joy extends ;
Sardinian mothers pay their vows fulfill'd ;
And hymns are heard beside thy banks,
O Fountain Arethuse !

9.

Churches shall blaze with lights, and ring with praise,
And deeper strains shall rise
From many an overflowing heart to Heaven ;
Nor will they in their prayers forget
The hand that set them free.

Keswick.

ODE

1.

DEATH has gone up into our Palaces !
The light of day once more
Hath visited the last abode
Of mortal royalty,
The dark and silent vault.

2.

But not as when the silence of that vault
Was interrupted last
Doth England raise her loud lament,
Like one by sudden grief
Surprised and overcome.

3.

Then with a passionate sorrow we bewail'd
Youth on the untimely bier ;
And hopes which seem'd like flower-buds full,
Just opening to the sun,
For ever swept away.

4.

The heart then struggled with repining thoughts,
With feelings that almost
Arraign'd the inscrutable decree,
Embittered by a sense
Of that which might have been.

5.

This grief hath no repining ; all is well,
What hath been, and what is.
The Angel of Deliverance came
To one who full of years
Awaited her release.

6.

All that our fathers in their prayers desired,
When first their chosen Queen
Set on our shores her happy feet,
All by indulgent Heaven
Had largely been vouchsafed.

7.

At Court the Household Virtues had their place;
Domestic Purity
Maintain'd her proper influence there :
The marriage bed was blest,
And length of days was given.

8.

No cause for sorrow then, but thankfulness ;
Life's business well perform'd,
When weary age full willingly
Resigns itself to sleep,
In sure and certain hope !

9.

Oh end to be desired, whene'er, as now,
Good works have gone before,
The seasonable fruit of Faith ;
And good Report, and good
Example have survived.

10.

Her left hand knew not of the ample alms
Which her right hand had done;
And therefore in the aweful hour,
The promises were hers
To secret bounty made.

11.

With more than royal honours to the tomb
Her bier is borne ; with more
Than Pomp can claim, or Power bestow ;
With blessings and with prayers
From many a grateful heart.

12.

Long, long then shall Queen Charlotte's name be
dear ;
And future Queens to her
As to their best examplar look ;
Who imitates her best
May best deserve our love.

Keswick, 1818.

ODE

FOR ST. GEORGE'S DAY.

1.

WILD were the tales which fabling monks of old
Devised to swell their hero's holy fame,
When in the noble army they enroll'd
St. George's doubtful name.
Of arrows and of spears they told
Which fell rebated from his mortal mould;
And how the burning fiery furnace blast
To him came tempered like a summer breeze,
When at the hour of evening it hath past
O'er gurgling tanks, and groves of lemon trees:
And how the reverential flame
Condensing like a garb of honour, play'd
In gorgeous folds around his glorious frame;
And how the Heathen in their frantic strife
With water then alike in vain, essay'd
His inextinguishable life.

2.

What marvel if the Christian Knight
Thus for his dear Redeemer's sake
Defied the purpled Pagan's might?
Such boldness well might he partake,

For he beside the Libyan lake
Silene, with the Infernal King
Had coped in actual fight.
The old Dragon on terrific wing
Assail'd him there with Stygian sting
And arrowy tongue, and potent breath
Exhaling pestilence and death.
Dauntless in faith the Champion stood,
Opposed against the rage of Hell
The Red-Cross shield, and wielding well
His sword, the strife pursued;
First with a wide and rending wound
Brought the maim'd monster to the ground,
Then pressing with victorious heel
Upon his scaly neck subdued,
Plunged and replunged the searching steel;
Till from the shameful overthrow
Howling the incarnate Demon fled,
And left that form untenanted,
And hid in Hell his humbled head,
Still trembling in the realm below,
At thought of that tremendous foe.

3.

Such tales monastic fablers taught;
Their kindred strain the minstrels caught;
A web of finer texture they
Wrought in the rich romantic lay;
Of magic caves and woods they sung,
Where Kalyb nursed the boy divine,
And how those woods and caverns rung
With cries from many a demon tongue,

When breaking from the witch's cell,
He bound her in her own strong spell.
And of the bowers of Ormandine
Where thrall'd by art, St. David lay
Sleeping inglorious years away,
Till our St. George, with happier arm
Released him, and dissolved the charm.
But most the minstrels loved to tell
Of that portentous day,
When Sabra at the stake was bound,
Her brow with sweetest garlands crown'd
The Egyptian Dragon's prey;
And how for her the English Knight,
Invincible at such a sight,
Engaged that fiendish beast in fight,
And o'er the monster, triple-scaled,
The good sword Askalon prevail'd.

4.

Such legends monks and minstrels feign'd,
And easily the wondrous tales obtain'd,
In those dark days, belief;
Shrines to the Saint were rear'd, and temples rose,
And states and kingdoms for their patron chose
The Cappadocian Chief.
Full soon his sainted name hath won
In fields of war a wide renown;
Spain saw the Moors confounded fly,
Before the well known slaughter cry,
St. George for Aragon!
And when the Catalans pursued
Their vengeful way with fire and blood,

The Turk and treacherous Greek were dearly taught
  That all-appalling shout,
 For them with rage and ruin fraught
  In many a dolorous rout.
'Twas in this heavenly Guardian's trusted strength,
 That Malta's old heroic knights defied
 The Ottoman in all his power and pride.
Repulsed from her immortal walls at length
The baffled Misbeliever turn'd with shame;
And when in after years in dreams he heard
That all-too-well remembered battle-word,
Woke starting at St. George's dreadful name,
And felt cold sweats of fear suffuse his trembling
    frame.

5.

But thou, O England! to that sainted name
Hast given its proudest praise, its loftiest fame.
 Witness the field of Cressy, on that day,
When vollying thunders roll'd unheard on high,
  For in that memorable fray,
 Broken, confused, and scatter'd in dismay,
France had ears only for the Conqueror's cry,
St. George, St. George for England! St. George
   and Victory!
Bear witness Poictiers! where again the foe
From that same hand received his overthrow.
In vain essay'd, Mont Joye St. Denis rang
  From many a boastful tongue,
And many a hopeful heart in onset brave;
Their courage in the shock of battle quail'd
His dread response, when sable Edward gave,
And England and St. George again prevail'd.

s 3

Bear witness Agincourt, where once again
The bannered lilies on the ensanguin'd plain
Were trampled by the fierce pursuers' feet;
And France, doom'd ever to defeat
Against that foe, beheld her myriads fly
Before the withering cry,
St. George, St. George for England! St. George
and Victory!

6.

That cry in many a field of Fame
Through glorious ages held its high renown;
Nor less hath Britain proved the sacred name
Auspicious to her crown.
Troubled too oft her course of fortune ran,
Till when the Georges came
Her happiest age began.
Beneath their just and liberal sway,
Old feuds and factions died away;
One feeling through her realms was known,
One interest of the Nation and the Throne.
Ring, then, ye bells upon St. George's Day,
From every tower in glad accordance ring;
And let all instruments full, strong, or sweet,
With touch of modulated string,
And soft or swelling breath, and sonorous beat,
The happy name repeat,
While heart and voice their joyous tribute bring
And speak the People's love for George their King.

Keswick, 1820.

ODE

WRITTEN AFTER THE KING'S VISIT TO IRELAND.

1.

How long, O Ireland, from thy guilty ground
Shall innocent blood
Arraign the inefficient arm of Power?
How long shall Murder there,
Leading his banded ruffians through the land,
Range unrepress'd?
How long shall Night
Bring to thy harmless dwellers, in the stead
Of natural rest, the feverish sleep of fear,
Midnight alarms,
Horrible dreams, and worse realities?
How long shall darkness cover, and the eye
Of Morning open upon deeds of death?

2.

In vain art thou by liberal Nature's dower
Exuberantly blest;
The Seasons in their course
Shed o'er thy hills and vales
The bounties of a genial clime, in vain;
Heaven hath in vain bestowed
Well-tempered liberty,
(Its last and largest boon to social man,)
If the brute Multitude from age to age,

s 4

Wild as their savage ancestors,
Go irreclaim'd the while,
From sire to son transmitting still
In undisturb'd descent,
(A sad inheritance!)
Their errors, and their crimes.

3.

Green Island of the West!
Thy Sister Kingdom fear'd not this
When thine exultant shores
Rung far and wide of late,
And grateful Dublin first beheld her King,
First of thy Sovereigns he
Who visited thy shores in peace and joy.

4.

Oh what a joy was there!
In loud huzzahs prolong'd,
Surge after surge the tide
Of popular welcome rose;
And in the intervals alone
Of that tumultuous sound of glad acclaim,
Could the deep cannon's voice
Of duteous gratulation, though it spake
In thunder, reach the ear.
From every tower the merry bells rung round,
Peal hurrying upon peal,
Till with the still reverberating din
The walls and solid pavement seem'd to shake,
And every bosom with the tremulous air
Inhaled a dizzy joy.

5.

Age that came forth to gaze,
That memorable day
Felt in its quicken'd veins a pulse like youth;
And lisping babes were taught to bless their King;
And grandsires bade the children treasure up
The precious sight, for it would be a tale
The which in their old age
Would make their children's children gather round
Intent, all ears to hear.

6.

Were then the feelings of that generous time
Ephemeral as the joy?
Pass'd they away like summer clouds,
Like dreams of infancy,
Like glories of the evening firmament,
Which fade, and leave no trace?
Merciful Heaven, oh let not thou the hope
Be frustrate, that our Sister Isle may reap
From the good seed then sown
Full harvests of prosperity and peace;
That perfect union may derive its date
From that auspicious day,
And equitable ages thence
Their lasting course begin;

7.

Green Island of the West,
While frantic violence delays
That happier order, still must thou remain
In thine own baleful darkness wrapt;

As if the Eye divine,
That which beholdeth all, from thee alone
In wrath had turn'd away!

8.

But not for ever thus shalt thou endure,
To thy reproach, and ours,
Thy misery, and our shame!
For Mercy shall go forth
To stablish Order, with an arm'd right hand;
And firm Authority
With its all-present strength controul the bad,
And with its all-sufficient shield
Protect the innocent:
The first great duty this of lawful Power
Which holds its delegated right from Heaven.

9.

The first great duty this; but this not all;
For more than comes within the scope
Of Power, is needed here;
More than to watch insidious discontent,
Curb, and keep curb'd the treasonable tongue,
And quell the madden'd multitude:
Labours of love remain;
To weed out noxious customs rooted deep
In a rank soil, and long left seeding there;
Pour balm into old wounds, and bind them up;
Remove remediable ills,
Improve the willing mind,
And win the generous heart.
Afflicted Country, from thyself

Must this redemption come;
And thou hast children able to perform
This work of faith and hope.

10.

O for a voice that might recall
To their deserted hearths
Thy truant sons! a voice
Whose virtuous cogency
Might with the strength of duty reach their souls;
A strength that should compel entire consent,
And to their glad obedience give
The impulse and the force of free good-will!
For who but they can knit
The severed links of that appointed chain,
Which when in just cohesion it unites
Order to order, rank to rank,
In mutual benefit,
So binding heart to heart,
It then connecteth Earth with Heaven, from whence
The golden links depend.

11.

Nor when the war is waged
With Error, and the brood
Of Darkness, will your aid
Be wanting in the cause of Light and Love,
Ye Ministers of that most holy Church
Whose firm foundations on the rock
Of Scripture rest secure!
What though the Romanist in numbers strong,
In misdirected zeal

And bigotry's blind force,
Assail your Fortress ; though the sons of Schism
Join in insane alliance with that old
Inveterate enemy,
Weening thereby to wreak
Their covenanted hatred, and effect
Your utter overthrow ;
What though the unbelieving crew,
For fouler purpose aid the unnatural league ;
And Faction's wolfish pack
Set up their fiercest yell, to augment
The uproar of assault ;
Clad in your panoply will ye be found,
Wielding the spear of Reason, with the sword
Of Scripture girt ; and from your shield of Truth
Such radiance shall go forth,
As when, unable to sustain its beams
On Arthur's arm unveil'd,
Earth-born Orgoglio reel'd, as if with wine ;
And from her many-headed beast cast down
Duessa fell, her cup of sorcery spilt,
Her three-crown'd mitre in the dust devolved,
And all her secret filthiness exposed.

12.

O thou fair Island, with thy Sister Isle
Indissolubly link'd for weal and woe ;
Partaker of her present power,
Her everlasting fame ;
Dear pledges hast thou render'd and received
Of that eternal union ! Bedell's grave
Is in thy keeping ; and with thee

Deposited, doth Taylor's holy dust
Await the Archangel's call.
O land profuse of genius and of worth,
Largely hast thou received, and largely given !

13.

Green Island of the West,
The example of unspotted Ormond's faith
To thee we owe ; to thee
Boyle's venerable name :
Berkeley the wise, the good :
And that great Orator who first
Unmask'd the harlot sorceress Anarchy,
What time, in Freedom's borrowed form profaned,
She to the nations round
Her draught of witchcraft gave :
And him who in the field
O'erthrow her giant offspring in his strength,
And brake the iron rod.
Proud of such debt,
Rich to be thus indebted, these,
Fair Island, Sister Queen
Of Ocean, Ireland, these to thee we owe.

14.

Shall I then imprecate
A curse on them that would divide
Our union ? .. Far be this from me, O Lord !
Far be it ! What is man,
That he should scatter curses ? .. King of Kings,
Father of all, Almighty, Governor
Of all things ! unto Thee

Humbly I offer up our holier prayer!
I pray Thee, not in wrath
But in thy mercy, to confound
These men's devices. Lord!
Lighten their darkness with thy Gospel light,
And thus abate their pride,
Assuage their malice thus!

Keswick, 1821.

ODE

1.

At length hath Scotland seen
The presence long desired;
The pomp of royalty
Hath gladden'd once again
Her ancient palace, desolate how long !
From all parts far and near,
Highland and lowland, glen and fertile carse,
The silent mountain lake, the busy port,
Her populous cities, and her pastoral hills,
In generous joy convened
By the free impulse of the loyal heart
Her sons have gather'd, and beheld their King.

2.

Land of the loyal, as in happy hour
Revisited, so was thy regal seat
In happy hour for thee
Forsaken, under favouring stars, when James
His valediction gave,
And great Eliza's throne
Received its rightful heir,
The Peaceful and the Just.

3.

A more auspicious union never Earth
From eldest days had seen,
Than when, their mutual wrongs forgiven,
And gallant enmity renounced
With honour, as in honour foster'd long,
The ancient Kingdoms formed
Their everlasting league.

4.

Slowly by time matured
A happier order then for Scotland rose;
And where inhuman force,
And rapine unrestrain'd
Had lorded o'er the land,
Peace came, and polity,
And quiet industry, and frugal wealth ;
And there the household virtues fix'd
Their sojourn undisturb'd.

5.

Such blessings for her dowry Scotland drew
From that benignant union; nor less large
The portion that she brought.
She brought security and strength,
True hearts, and strenuous hands, and noble minds.
Say, Ocean, from the shores of Camperdown,
What Caledonia brought!   Say thou,
Egypt !   Let India tell !
And let tell Victory
From that Brabantine field,
The proudest field of fame !

6.

Speak ye, too, Works of peace ;
For ye too have a voice
Which shall be heard by ages! The proud Bridge,
Through whose broad arches, worthy of their name
And place, his rising and his refluent tide
Majestic Thames, the royal river rolls ;
And that which high in air
A bending line suspended, shall o'erhang
Menai's straits, as if
By Merlin's mighty magic there sustain'd ;
And Pont-Cyssylté, not less wondrous work ;
Where on gigantic columns raised
Aloft, a dizzying height,
The laden barge pursues its even way,
While o'er his rocky channel the dark Dee
Hurries below, a raging stream, scarce heard.
And that huge mole, whose deep foundations, firm
As if by Nature laid,
Repel the assailing billows, and protect
The British fleet, securely riding there,
Though southern storms possess the sea and sky,
And from its depths commoved,
Infuriate ocean raves.
Ye stately monuments of Britain's power,
Bear record ye what Scottish minds
Have plann'd and perfected !
With grateful wonder shall posterity
See the stupendous works, and Rennie's name,
And Telford's shall survive, till time
Leave not a wreck of sublunary things.

7.

Him too may I attest for Scotland's praise,
Who seized and wielded first
The mightiest element
That lies within the scope of man's controul ;
Of evil and of good,
Prolific spring, and dimly yet discern'd
The immeasurable results.
The mariner no longer seeks
Wings from the wind ; creating now the power
Wherewith he wins his way,
Right on across the ocean-flood he steers
Against opposing skies ;
And reaching now the inmost continent,
Up rapid streams, innavigable else,
Ascends with steady progress, self-propell'd.

8.

Nor hath the Sister kingdom borne
In science and in arms
Alone, her noble part ;
There is an empire which survives
The wreck of thrones, the overthrow of realms,
The downfall, and decay, and death
Of Nations. Such an empire in the mind
Of intellectual man
Rome yet maintains, and elder Greece, and such
By indefeasible right
Hath Britain made her own.
How fair a part doth Caledonia claim
In that fair conquest ! Whereso'er
The British tongue may spread,

(A goodly tree, whose leaf
No winter e'er shall nip ;)
Earthly immortals, there, her sons of fame,
Will have their heritage.
In eastern and in occidental Ind ;
The new antarctic world, where sable swans
Glide upon waters, call'd by British names,
And plough'd by British keels ;
In vast America through all its length
And breadth, from Massachusett's populous coast
To western Oregan;
And from the southern gulph,
Where the great river with his turbid flood
Stains the green Ocean, to the polar sea.

9.

There nations yet unborn shall trace
In Hume's perspicuous page,
How Britain rose, and through what storms attain'd
Her eminence of power.
In other climates, youths and maidens there
Shall learn from Thomson's verse in what attire
The various seasons, bringing in their change
Variety of good,
Revisit their beloved English ground.
There Beattie ! in thy sweet and soothing strain
Shall youthful poets read
Their own emotions. There too, old and young,
Gentle and simple, by Sir Walter's tales
Spell-bound shall feel
Imaginary hopes and fears
T 2

Strong as realities,
And waking from the dream, regret its close.

10.

These Scotland are thy glories ; and thy praise
Is England's, even as her power
And opulence of fame are thine.
So hath our happy union made
Each in the other's weal participant,
Enriching, strengthening, glorifying both.

11.

O House of Stuart, to thy memory still
For this best benefit
Should British hearts in gratitude be bound !
A deeper tragedy
Than thine unhappy tale hath never fill'd
The historic page, nor given
Poet or moralist his mournful theme.
O House severely tried,
And in prosperity alone
Found wanting, Time hath closed
Thy tragic story now !
Errors, and virtues fatally betrayed,
Magnanimous suffering, vice,
Weakness, and head-strong zeal, sincere, tho' blind,
Wrongs, calumnies, heart-wounds,
Religious resignation, earthly hopes,
Fears and affections, these have had their course,
And over them in peace
The all-ingulphing stream of years hath closed.

But this good work endures,
'Stablish'd and perfected by length of days,
The indissoluble union stands.

12.
Nor hath the sceptre from that line
Departed, though the name hath lost
Its regal honours.   Trunk and root have fail'd:
A scion from the stock
Liveth and flourisheth.   It is the Tree
Beneath whose sacred shade,
In majesty and peaceful power serene,
The Island Queen of Ocean hath her seat;
Whose branches far and near
Extend their sure protection; whose strong roots
Are with the Isle's foundations inter-knit;
Whose stately summit when the storm careers
Below, abides unmoved,
Safe in the sunshine and the peace of Heaven.

Keswick, 1822.

THE WARNING VOICE.

THE WARNING VOICE.

ODE I.

1.

Take up thy prophecy,
Thou dweller in the mountains, who hast nursed
Thy soul in solitude,
Holding communion with immortal minds,
Poets and Sages of the days of old;
And with the sacred food
Of meditation and of lore divine
Hast fed thy heavenly part;
Take up thy monitory strain.
O son of song, a strain severe
Of warning and of woe!

2.

O Britain, O my Mother Isle,
Ocean's imperial Queen,
Thou glory of all lands!
Is there a curse upon thee, that thy sons
Would rush to ruin, drunk
With sin, and in infuriate folly blind?
Hath Hell enlarged itself,
And are the Fiends let loose
To work thine overthrow?

3.

For who is she
That on the many-headed Beast
Triumphantly enthroned,
Doth ride abroad in state,
The Book of her Enchantments in her hand ?
Her robes are stain'd with blood,
And on her brazen front
Is written BLASPHEMY.

4.

Know ye not then the Harlot ? know ye not
Her shameless forehead, her obdurate eye,
Her meretricious mien,
Her loose immodest garb with slaughter foul ?
Your Fathers knew her ; when delirious France,
Drunk with her witcheries,
Upon the desecrated altar set
The Sorceress, and with rites
Inhuman and accurst,
O'er all the groaning land
Perform'd her sacrifice.

5.

Your Fathers knew her ! when the nations round
Received her maddening spell,
And call'd her Liberty,
And in that name proclaim'd
A jubilee for guilt ;
When their blaspheming hosts defied high Heaven,
And wheresoe'er they went let havoc loose ;
Your Fathers knew the Sorceress ! They stood firm

And in that hour of trial faithful found,
They raised the Red Cross flag.

6.

They knew her; and they knew
That not in scenes of rapine and of blood,
In lawless riotry,
And wallowing with the multitude obscene,
Would Liberty be found!
Her in her form divine,
Her genuine form they knew;
For Britain was her home,
With Order and Religion there she dwelt;
It was her chosen seat,
Her own beloved Isle.
Think not that Liberty
From Order and Religion e'er will dwell
Apart; companions they
Of heavenly seed connate.

7.

Woe, woe for Britain, woe!
If that society divine,
By lewd and impious uproar driven,
Indignantly should leave
The land that in their presence hath been blest!
Woe, woe! for in her streets
Should grey-hair'd Polity
Be trampled under foot by ruffian force;
And Murder to the noon-day sky
Lift his red hands, as if no God were there
War would lay waste the realm;

Devouring fire consume
Temples and Palaces ;
Nor would the lowliest cot
Escape that indiscriminating storm,
When Heaven upon the guilty nation pour'd
The vials of its wrath.

8.

These are no doubtful ills !
The unerring voice of Time
Warns us that what hath been again shall be ;
And the broad beacon-flame
Of History, casts its light
Upon Futurity.

9.

Turn not thy face away,
Almighty ! from the realm
By thee so highly favoured, and so long.
Thou who in war hast been our shield and strength,
From famine who hast saved us, and hast bade
The Earthquake and the Pestilence go by,
Spare us, O Father ! save us from ourselves !
From insane Faction, who prepares the pit
In which itself would fall ;
From rabid Treason's rage, . .
The poor priest-ridden Papist's erring zeal, . .
The lurking Atheist's wiles, . .
The mad Blasphemer's venom, . . from our foes,
Our follies and our errors, and our sins,
Save us, O Father ! for thy mercy's sake,
Thou who ALONE canst save !

Keswick, 1819.

THE WARNING VOICE.

ODE II.

1.

In a vision I was seized,
When the elements were hush'd
In the stillness that is felt
Ere the Storm goes abroad;
Thro' the air I was borne away
And in spirit I beheld
Where a City lay beneath,
Like a valley mapp'd below,
When seen from a mountain top.

2.

The night had closed around,
And o'er the sullen sky
Were the wide wings of darkness spread,
The City's myriad lamps
Shone mistily below,
Like stars in the bosom of a lake;
And its murmurs arose
Incessant and deep,
Like the sound of the sea
Where it rakes on a stoney shore.

3.

A voice from the darkness went forth,
" Son of Man, look below !
This is the City to be visited ;
For as a fountain
Casteth its waters,
So casteth she her wickedness abroad !"
Mine eyes were opened then,
And the veil which conceals
The Invisible World was withdrawn.

4.

I look'd, and behold !
As the Patriarch, in his dream,
Saw the Angels to and fro
Pass from Heaven to Earth,
On their ministry of love ;
So saw I where a way
From that great City, led
To the black abyss of bale,
To the dolorous region of Death.

5.

Wide and beaten was the way,
And deep the descent
To the Adamantine Gates,
Which were thrown on their hinges back.
Wailing and Woe were within,
And the gleam of sulphurous fires,
In darkness and smoke involved.

6.

And through those open gates
The Fiends were swarming forth ;
Hastily, joyfully,
As to a jubilee,
The Spirits accurst were trooping up :
They fill'd the streets,
And they bore with them curses and plagues ;
And they scatter'd lies abroad,
Horrors, obscenities,
Blasphemies, treasons,
And the seeds of strife and death.

7.

" Son of Man, look up ! " said the Voice.
I look'd and beheld
The way which Angels tread,
Seen like a pillar of light
That slants from a broken sky.
That heavenly way by clouds was closed,
Heavy, and thick, and dark, with thunder charged
And there a Spirit stood,
Who raised in menacing act his aweful arm ;
He spake aloud, and thrill'd
My inmost soul with fear.

8.

" Woe ! Woe !
Woe to the City where Faction reigns !
Woe to the Land where Sedition prevails !
Woe to the Nation whom Hell deceives !
Woe ! Woe !

They have Eyes, and they will not see!
They have Ears, and they will not hear!
They have Hearts, and they will not feel!
Woe to the People who fasten their eyes!
Woe to the People who deafen their ears!
Woe to the People who harden their hearts!
Woe! Woe!
The Vials are charged;
The measure is full;
The wrath is ripe;..
Woe! Woe!"

9.
But from that City then, behold,
A gracious form arose;
Her snow-white wings upon the dusky air
Shone like the waves that glow
Around a midnight keel in liquid light.
Upward her supplicating arms were spread
And as her face to heaven
In eloquent grief she raised,
Loose, like a Comet's refluent tresses, hung
Her heavenly hair dispersed.

10.
" Not yet, O Lord! not yet,
O merciful as just!
Not yet!".. the Tutelary Angel cried;
" For I must plead with thee for this poor land,
Guilty,.. but still the seat
Of genuine piety,..
The mother still of noble minds, ..

The nurse of high desires !
Not yet, O Lord, not yet,
Give thou thine anger way!
Thou who hast set thy Bow
Of Mercy in the clouds
Not yet, O Lord, pour out
The Vials of thy wrath !

11.

" Oh, for the sake
Of that religion pure and undefiled
Here purchased by thy Martyrs' precious blood, ..
Mercy, Oh mercy, Lord !
For that well-order'd frame of equal laws,
Time's goodliest monument,
O'er which thy guardian shield
So oft hath been extended heretofore, ..
Mercy, Oh mercy, Lord !
For the dear charities
The household virtues, that in secret there,
Like sweetest violets, send their fragrance forth,
Mercy, Oh mercy, Lord !

12.

" Oh wilt thou quench the light,
That should illuminate
The nations who in darkness sit,
And in the shadow of death ? ..
Oh wilt thou stop the heart
Of intellectual life ? ..
Wilt thou seel the eye of the world ? ..
Mercy, Oh mercy, Lord !

13.

" Not for the guilty few ;
Nor for the erring multitude,
The ignorant many, wickedly misled, . .
Send thou thy vengeance down
Upon a land so long the dear abode
Of Freedom, Knowledge, Virtue, Faith, approved, .
Thine own beloved land !
Oh let not Hell prevail
Against her past deserts, . .
Against her actual worth . .
Against her living hopes, . .
Against the Prayers that rise
From righteous hearts this hour !

14.

" Plead with me, O ye Dead ! whose sacred dust
Is laid in hope within her hallow'd soil,
Plead with me for your Country, suffering now
Beneath such loathsome plagues,
As ancient Egypt in her slime
And hot corruption bred.
Plead with me at this hour
All wise and upright Minds,
All honourable Hearts, . .
For ye abhor the sins
Which, o'er the guilty land,
Have drawn this gather'd storm !
Plead with me Souls unborn,
Ye who are doomed upon this fateful spot
To pass your pilgrimage,
Earth's noblest heritors.

Or children of a ruin'd realm, to shame
And degradation born, ..
(For this is on the issue of the hour!)
Plead with me, unborn Spirits! that the wrath
Deserved, may pass away!

15.

" Join in my supplication, Seas and Lands, ..
I call upon you all!
Thou, Europe, in whose cause,
Alone and undismay'd,
The generous nation strove;
For whose deliverance in the Spanish fields
Her noblest blood was pour'd
Profusely; and on that Brabantine plain,
(The proudest fight that e'er
By virtuous victory
Was hallowed to all time.)
Join, with me, Africa!
For here hath thy redemption had its birth; ..
Thou, India, who art blest
With peace and equity
Beneath her easy sway; ..
And thou, America, who owest
The large and inextinguishable debt
Of filial love! .. And ye,
Remote Antarctic Isles and Continent,
Where the glad tidings of the Gospel truth,
Her children are proclaiming faithfully;
Join with me now to wrest
The thunderbolt from that relenting arm! ..
Plead with me, Earth and Ocean, at this hour,

Thou, Ocean, for thy Queen,
And for thy benefactress, thou, O Earth !"

16.
The Angel ceased ;
The vision fled ;
The wind arose,
The clouds were rent,
They were drifted and scatter'd abroad ;
And as I look'd, and saw
Where through the clear blue sky the silver Moon
Moved in her light serene,
A healing influence reach'd my heart,
And I felt in my soul
That the voice of the Angel was heard.

Keswick, 1820.

ODE

ON

THE PORTRAIT OF BISHOP HEBER.

ODE

ON THE PORTRAIT OF BISHOP HEBER.

1.

YES,.. such as these were Heber's lineaments ;
Such his capacious front,
His comprehensive eye,
His open brow serene.
Such was the gentle countenance which bore
Of generous feeling, and of golden truth,
Sure Nature's sterling impress ; never there
Unruly passion left
Its ominous marks infix'd,
Nor the worse die of evil habit set
An inward stain ingrain'd.
Such were the lips whose salient playfulness
Enliven'd peaceful hours of private life ;
Whose eloquence
Held congregations open-ear'd,
As from the heart it flow'd, a living stream
Of Christian wisdom, pure and undefiled.

2.

And what if there be those
Who in the cabinet
Of memory hold enshrined
A livelier portraiture,
And see in thought, as in their dreams,

u 4

His actual image, verily produced ;
Yet shall this counterfeit convey
To strangers, and preserve for after-time,
All that could perish of him, . . all that else
Even now had past away :
For he hath taken with the Living Dead
His honourable place, . .
Yea, with the Saints of God
His holy habitation.   Hearts, to which
Thro' ages he shall speak,
Will yearn towards him ; and they too, (for such
Will be,) who gird their loins
With truth to follow him,
Having the breast-plate on of righteousness,
The helmet of salvation, and the shield
Of faith, . . they too will gaze
Upon his effigy
With reverential love,
'Till they shall grow familiar with its lines,
And know him when they see his face in Heaven.

3.

Ten years have held their course
Since last I look'd upon
That living countenance,
When on Llangedwin's terraces we paced
Together, to and fro.
Partaking there its hospitality,
We with its honoured master spent,
Well-pleased, the social hours ;
His friend and mine, . . my earliest friend, whom I
Have ever, thro' all changes, found the same,

From boyhood to grey hairs,
In goodness, and in worth and warmth of heart.
Together then we traced
The grass-grown site, where armed feet once trod
The threshold of Glendower's embattled hall;
Together sought Melangel's lonely Church,
Saw the dark yews, majestic in decay,
Which in their flourishing strength
Cyveilioc might have seen;
Letter by letter traced the lines
On Yorwerth's fabled tomb;
And curiously observed what vestiges,
Mouldering and mutilate,
Of Monacella's legend there are left,
A tale humane, itself
Well-nigh forgotten now:
Together visited the ancient house
Which from the hill-slope takes
Its Cymric name euphonious; there to view,
Tho' drawn by some rude limner inexpert,
The faded portrait of that lady fair,
Beside whose corpse her husband watch'd,
And with perverted faith,
Preposterously placed,
Thought, obstinate in hopeless hope, to see
The beautiful dead, by miracle, revive.

4.

The sunny recollections of those days
Full soon were overcast, when Heber went
Where half this wide world's circle lay
Between us interposed.

A messenger of love he went,
A true Evangelist;
Not for ambition, nor for gain,
Nor of constraint, save such as duty lays
Upon the disciplin'd heart,
Took he the overseeing on himself,
Of that wide flock dispers'd,
Which, till these latter times,
Had there been left to stray
Neglected all too long.
For this great end devotedly he went,
Forsaking friends and kin,
His own loved paths of pleasantness and peace,
Books, leisure, privacy,
Prospects (and not remote), of all wherewith
Authority could dignify desert;
And, dearer far to him,
Pursuits that with the learned and the wise
Should have assured his name its lasting place.

5.

Large, England, is the debt
Thou owest to Heathendom;
To India most of all, where Providence,
Giving thee thy dominion there in trust,
Upholds its baseless strength.
All seas have seen thy red-cross flag
In war triumphantly display'd;
Late only has thou set that standard up
On pagan shores in peace !
Yea, at this hour the cry of blood
Riseth against thee from beneath the wheels

Of that seven-headed Idol's car accurst ;
Against thee, from the widow's funeral pile
The smoke of human sacrifice
Ascends, even now, to Heaven !

6.

The debt shall be discharged ; the crying sin
Silenced ; the foul offence
For ever done away.
Thither our saintly Heber went,
In promise and in pledge
That England, from her guilty torpor roused,
Should zealously and wisely undertake
Her aweful task assign'd :
Thither, devoted to the work, he went,
There spent his precious life,
There left his holy dust.

7.

How beautiful are the feet of him
That bringeth good tidings,
That publisheth peace,
That bringeth good tidings of good,
That proclaimeth salvation for men
Where'er the Christian Patriarch went,
Honour and reverence heralded his way,
And blessings followed him.
The Malabar, the Moor, the Cingalese,
Tho' unillumed by faith,
Yet not the less admired
The virtue that they saw.
The European soldier, there so long

Of needful and consolatory rites
Injuriously deprived,
Felt, at his presence, the neglected seed
Of early piety
Refresh'd, as with a quickening dew from Heaven.
Native believers wept for thankfulness,
When on their heads he laid his hallowing hands;
And, if the Saints in bliss
Be cognizant of aught that passeth here,
It was a joy for Schwartz
To look from Paradise that hour
Upon his earthly flock.

8

Ram boweth down,
Creeshna and Seeva stoop;
The Arabian Moon must wane to wax no more :
And Ishmael's seed redeem'd,
And Esau's .. to their brotherhood,
And to their better birthright then restored,
Shall within Israel's covenant be brought.
Drop down, ye Heavens, from above!
Ye Skies, pour righteousness !
Open, thou Earth, and let
Salvation be brought forth !
And sing ye, O ye Heavens, and shout, O Earth,
With all thy hills and vales,
Thy mountains and thy woods,
Break forth into a song, a jubilant song,
For by Himself the Lord hath sworn
That every tongue to Him shall swear,
, To Him that every knee shall bow.

9.

Take comfort, then, my soul!
Thy latter days on earth,
Tho' few, shall not be evil, by this hope
Supported, and enlighten'd on the way.
O Reginald, one course,
Our studies, and our thoughts,
Our aspirations held,
Wherein, but mostly in this blessed hope,
We had a bond of union, closely knit
In spirit, though in this world's wilderness
Apart our lots were cast.
Seldom we met; but I knew well
That whatsoe'er this never-idle hand
Sent forth would find with thee
Benign acceptance, to its full desert.
For thou wert of that audience, .. fit, though few,
For whom I am content
To live laborious days,
Assured that after years will ratify
Their honourable award.

10.

Hadst thou revisited thy native land,
Mortality and Time,
And Change, must needs have made
Our meeting mournful.   Happy he
Who to his rest is borne
In sure and certain hope,
Before the hand of age
Hath chill'd his faculties,
Or sorrow reach'd him in his heart of hearts!

Most happy if he leave in his good name
A light for those who follow him,
And in his works a living seed
Of good, prolific still.

11.

Yes, to the Christian, to the Heathen world,
Heber, thou art not dead, .. thou canst not die !
Nor can I think of thee as lost.
A little portion of this little isle
At first divided us ; then half the globe :
The same earth held us still ; but when,
O Reginald, wert thou so near as now !
'T is but the falling of a withered leaf, ..
The breaking of a shell, ..
The rending of a veil !
Oh when that leaf shall fall, ..
That shell be burst, .. that veil be rent, .. may then
My spirit be with thine !

Keswick, 1820.

EPISTLE

TO

ALLAN CUNNINGHAM.

TO ALLAN CUNNINGHAM.

WELL, Heaven be thank'd ! friend Allan, here I am,
Once more to that dear dwelling place return'd,
Where I have past the whole mid stage of life,
Not idly, certes ; not unworthily, ..
So let me hope : where Time upon my head
Hath laid his frore and monitory hand ;
And when this poor frail earthly tabernacle
Shall be dissolved, .. it matters not how soon
Or late, in God's good time, .. where I would fain
Be gathered to my children, earth to earth.

Needless it were to say how willingly
I bade the huge metropolis farewell,
Its din, and dust, and dirt, and smoke, and smut,
Thames' water, paviours' ground, and London sky ;
Weary of hurried days and restless nights,
Watchmen, whose office is to murder sleep
When sleep might else have weigh'd ones eyelids down,
Rattle of carriages, and roll of carts,
And tramp of iron hoofs ; and worse then all, ..
Confusion being worse confounded then,
With coachmen's quarrels and with footmen's shouts,
My next-door neighbours, in a street not yet
Macadamized, (me miserable !) *at home ;*
For then had we from midnight until morn

House-quakes, street-thunders, and door-batteries.
O Government! in thy wisdom and thy want,
Tax knockers;.. in compassion to the sick,
And those whose sober habits are not yet
Inverted, topsy-turvying night and day,
Tax them more heavily than thou hast charged
Armorial bearings and bepowder'd pates.
And thou, O Michael, ever to be praised,
Angelic among Taylors! for thy laws
Antifuliginous, extend those laws
Till every chimney its own smoke consume,
And give thenceforth thy dinners unlampoon'd.
Escaping from all this, the very whirl
Of mail-coach wheels bound outward from Lad-lane,
Was peace and quietness.   Three hundred miles
Of homeward way seem'd to the body rest,
And to the mind repose.

        Donne * did not hate
More perfectly that city.   Not for all
Its social, all its intellectual joys,..
Which having touch'd, I may not condescend
To name aught else the Demon of the place
Might for his lure hold forth;.. not even for these
Would I forego gardens and green-field walks,
And hedge-row trees, and stiles, and shady lanes,
And orchards, were such ordinary scenes

---

 * This poet begins his second Satire thus : —

  " Sir, though (I thank God for it) I do hate
   Perfectly all this town, yet there's one state
   In all ill things so excellently best,
   That hate towards them breeds pity towards the rest."

Alone to me accessible as those
Wherein I learnt in infancy to love
The sights and sounds of Nature ;.. wholesome sights
Gladdening the eye that they refresh ; and sounds
Which, when from life and happiness they spring,
Bear with them to the yet unharden'd heart
A sense that thrills its cords of sympathy ;
Or, when proceeding from insensate things,
Give to tranquillity a voice wherewith
To woo the ear and win the soul attuned ; ...
Oh not for all that London might bestow,
Would I renounce the genial influences
And thoughts and feelings to be found where'er
We breathe beneath the open sky, and see
Earth's liberal bosom.   Judge then by thyself,
Allan, true child of Scotland,.. thou who art
So oft in spirit on thy native hills,
And yonder Solway shores,.. a poet thou,
Judge by thyself how strong the ties which bind
A poet to his home ; when, .. making thus
Large recompense for all that haply else
Might seem perversely or unkindly done, ..
Fortune hath set his happy habitacle
Among the ancient hills, near mountain streams
And lakes pellucid, in a land sublime
And lovely as those regions of Romance
Where his young fancy in its day-dreams roam'd,
Expatiating in forests wild and wide,
Loëgrian, or of dearest Faery-land.

   Yet, Allan, of the cup of social joy
No man drinks freelier, nor with heartier **thirst,**

Nor keener relish, where I see around
Faces which I have known and loved so long,
That when he prints a dream upon my brain
Dan Morpheus takes them for his readiest types.
And therefore in that loathed metropolis
Time measured out to me some golden hours.
They were not leaden-footed while the clay
Beneath the patient touch of Chantrey's hand
Grew to the semblance of my lineaments.
Lit up in memory's landscape, like green spots
Of sunshine, are the mornings, when in talk
With him, and thee, and Bedford (my true friend
Of forty years,) I saw the work proceed,
Subject the while myself to no restraint,
But pleasureably in frank discourse engaged :
Pleased too, and with no unbecoming pride
To think this countenance, such as it is,
So oft by rascally mislikeness wrong'd,
Should faithfully to those who in his works
Have seen the inner man portray'd, be shown,
And in enduring marble should partake
Of our great sculptor's immortality.

I have been libell'd, Allan, as thou knowest,
Through all degrees of calumny ; but they
Who fix one's name for public sale beneath
A set of features slanderously unlike,
Are the worst libellers. Against the wrong
Which they inflict Time hath no remedy.
Injuries there are which Time redresseth best,
Being more sure in judgement, though perhaps
Slower in process even than the court

Where justice, tortoise-footed and mole-eyed,
Sleeps undisturb'd, fann'd by the lulling wings
Of harpies at their prey. We soon live down
Evil or good report, if undeserved.
Let then the dogs of Faction bark and bay,
Its bloodhounds, savaged by a cross of wolf,
Its full-bred kennel from the Blatant-beast ;
And from my lady's gay varanda, let
Her pamper'd lap-dog with his fetid breath
In bold bravado join, and snap and growl,
With petulant consequentialness elate,
There in his imbecility at once
Ridiculous and safe; though all give cry,
Whiggery's sleek spaniels, and its lurchers lean,
Its poodles by unlucky training marr'd,
Mongrel and cur and bob-tail, let them yelp
Till weariness and hoarseness shall at length
Silence the noisy pack; meantime be sure
I will not stoop for stones to cast among them.
The foumarts and the skunks may be secure
In their own scent; and for that viler swarm,
The vermin of the press, both those that skip,
And those that creep and crawl, I do not catch
And pin them for exposure on the page,
Their filth is their defence.
                But I appeal
Against the limner's and the graver's wrong;
Their evil works survive them. Bilderdijk,
Whom I am privileged to call my friend,
Suffering by graphic libels in likewise,
Gave his wrath vent in verse. Would I could give
The life and spirit of his vigorous Dutch,

As his dear consort hath transfused my strains
Into her native speech ; and made them known
On Rhine and Yssel, and rich Amstel's banks ;
And wheresoe'er the voice of Vondel still
Is heard, and still Antonides and Hooft
Are living agencies ; and Father Cats,
The household poet, teacheth in his songs
The love of all things lovely, all things pure :
Best poet, who delights the cheerful mind
Of childhood, stores with moral strength the heart
Of youth, with wisdom maketh mid-life rich,
And fills with quiet tears the eyes of age.

   Hear then in English rhyme how Bilderdijk
Describes his wicked portraits, one by one.

" A madman who from Bedlam hath broke loose ;
   An honest fellow of the numskull race ;
And pappyer-headed still, a very goose
   Staring with eyes aghast and vacant face ;
A Frenchman who would mirthfully display
   On some poor idiot his malicious wit ;
And lastly, one who, train'd up in the way
   Of worldly craft, hath not forsaken it,
But hath served Mammon with his whole intent,
   A thing of Nature's worst materials made,
Low-minded, stupid, base and insolent.
   I, .. I, .. a Poet, .. have been thus portray'd.
Can ye believe that my true effigy
   Among these vile varieties is found ?
What thought, or line, or word, hath fallen from me
   In all my numerous works whereon to ground

The opprobrious notion ?   Safely I may smile
  At these, acknowledging no likeness here.
But worse is yet to come ; so, soft awhile !
  For now in potter's earth must I appear,
And in such workmanship, that, sooth to say,
  Humanity disowns the imitation,
'And the dolt image is not worth its clay.
  Then comes there one who will to admiration
In plastic wax my perfect face present;
  And what of his performance comes at last ?
Folly itself in every lineament !
  Its consequential features overcast
With the coxcombical and shallow laugh
  Of one who would, for condescension, hide,
Yet in his best behaviour, can but half
  Suppress the scornfulness of empty pride."

  " And who is Bilderdijk ? " methinks thou sayest,
A ready question ; yet which, trust me, Allan,
Would not be ask'd, had not the curse that came
From Babel, clipt the wings of Poetry.
Napoleon ask'd him once with cold fix'd look,
" Art thou then in the world of letters known ? "
" I have deserved to be," the Hollander
Replied, meeting that proud imperial look
With calm and proper confidence, and eye
As little wont to turn away abash'd
Before a mortal presence.   He is one
Who hath received upon his constant breast
The sharpest arrows of adversity ;
Whom not the clamours of the multitude,
Demanding in their madness and their might

Iniquitous things, could shake in his firm mind ;
Nor the strong hand of instant tyranny,
From the straight path of duty turn aside.
But who in public troubles, in the wreck
Of his own fortunes, in proscription, exile,
Want, obloquy, ingratitude, neglect,
And what severer trials Providence
Sometimes inflicteth, chastening whom it loves,
In all, thro' all, and over all, hath borne
An equal heart, as resolute toward
The world, as humbly and religiously
Beneath his heavenly Father's rod resign d.
Right-minded, happy-minded, righteous man,
True lover of his country and his kind ;
In knowledge, and in inexhaustive stores
Of native genius rich ; philosopher,
Poet, and sage.   The language of a State
Inferior in illustrious deeds to none,
But circumscribed by narrow bounds, and now
Sinking in irrecoverable decline,
Hath pent within its sphere a name wherewith
Europe should else have rung from side to side.

    Such, Allan, is the Hollander to whom
Esteem and admiration have attach'd
My soul, not less than pre-consent of mind,
And gratitude for benefits, when being
A stranger, sick, and in a foreign land,
He took me like a brother to his house,
And ministered to me, and made a time
Which had been wearisome and careful else,
So pleasurable, that in my kalendar

There are no whiter days. 'T will be a joy
For us to meet in Heaven, tho' we should look
Upon each other's earthly face no more.
. . This is this world's complexion ! "cheerful thoughts
Bring sad thoughts to the mind," and these again
Give place to calm content, and steadfast hope,
And happy faith assured. . . Return we now,
With such transition as our daily life
Imposes in its wholesome discipline,
To a lighter strain ; and from the gallery
Of the Dutch Poet's mis-resemblances
Pass into mine ; where I shall show thee, Allan,
Such an array of villainous visages,
That if among them all there were but one
Which as a likeness could be proved upon me,
It were enough to make me in mere shame
Take up an alias, and forswear myself.

Whom have we first ?   A dainty gentleman,
His sleepy eyes half-closed, and countenance
To no expression stronger than might suit
A simper, capable of being moved :
Sawney and sentimental ; with an air
So lack-thought and so lackadaisycal,
You might suppose the volume in his hand
Must needs be Zimmermann on Solitude.

Then comes a jovial landlord, who hath made it
Part of his trade to be the shoeing horn
For his commercial customers.   God Bacchus
Hath not a thirstier votary.   Many a pipe
Of Porto's vintage hath contributed

To give his cheeks that deep carmine engrain'd,
And many a runlet of right Nantes, I ween,
Hath suffered percolation thro' that trunk,
Leaving behind it in the boozey eyes
A swoln and red suffusion, glazed and dim.

Our next is in the evangelical line,
A leaden-visaged specimen; demure,
Because he hath put on his Sunday's face;
Dull by formation, by complexion sad,
By bile, opinions, and dyspepsy sour.
One of the sons of Jack, .. I know not which,
For Jack hath a most numerous progeny, ..
Made up for Mr. Colburn's Magazine
This pleasant composite; a bust supplied
The features; look, expression, character
Are of the artist's fancy and free grace.
Such was that fellow's birth and parentage.
The rascal proved prolific; one of his breed,
By Docteur Pichot introduced in France,
Passes for Monsieur Sooté; and another, ..
An uglier miscreant too, .. the brothers Schumann
And their most cruel copper-scratcher Zschoch,
From Zwickau sent abroad through Germany.
I wish the Schumen and the copper-scratcher
No worse misfortune for their recompence,
Than to encounter such a cut-throat face
In the Black Forest or the Odenwald.,

And now is there a third derivative
From Mr. Colburn's composite, which late
The Arch-Pirate Galignani hath prefix'd,

A spurious portrait to a faithless life,
And bearing lyingly the libell'd name
Of Lawrence, impudently there insculpt.

　　The bust that was the innocent forefather
To all this base, abominable brood,
I blame not, Allan. 'T was the work of Smith,
A modest, mild, ingenious man, and errs,
Where erring, only because over-true,
Too close a likeness for similitude;
Fixing to every part and lineament
Its separate character, and missing thus
That which results from all.
　　　　　　　　　　Sir Smug comes next;
Allan, I own Sir Smug! I recognise
That visage with its dull sobriety;
I see it duly as the day returns,
When at the looking-glass with lather'd chin
And razor-weapon'd hand I sit, the face
Composed and apprehensively intent
Upon the necessary operation
About to be perform'd, with touch, alas,
Not always confident of hair-breadth skill.
Even in such sober sadness and constrain'd
Composure cold, the faithful Painter's eye
Had fix'd me like a spell, and I could feel
My features stiffen as he glanced upon them.
And yet he was a man whom I loved dearly,
My fellow-traveller, my familiar friend,
My household guest. But when he look'd upon me,
Anxious to exercise his excellent art,

The countenance he knew so thoroughly
Was gone, and in its stead there sate Sir Smug.

Under the graver's hand, Sir Smug became
Sir Smouch, .. a son of Abraham.   Now albeit,
Far rather would I trace my lineage thence
Than with the oldest line of Peers or Kings
Claim consanguinity, that cast of features
Would ill accord with me, who in all forms
Of pork, baked, roasted, toasted, boil'd or broil'd,
Fresh, salted, pickled, seasoned, moist or dry,
Whether ham, bacon, sausage, souse or brawn,
Leg, bladebone, baldrib, griskin, chine, or chop,
Profess myself a genuine Philopig.

It was, however, as a Jew whose portion
Had fallen unto him in a goodly land
Of loans, of omnium, and of three per cents,
That Messrs. Percy of the Anecdote-firm
Presented me unto their customers.
Poor Smouch endured a worse judaization
Under another hand.   In this next stage
He is on trial at the Old Bailey, charged
With dealing in base coin.   That he is guilty
No Judge or Jury could have half a doubt
When they saw the culprit's face; and he himself,
As you may plainly see, is comforted
By thinking he has just contrived to keep
Out of rope's reach, and will come off this time
For transportation.
                              Stand thou forth for trial,
Now, William Darton, of the Society

Of Friends called Quakers; thou who in 4th month
Of the year 24, on Holborn Hill,
At No. 58., didst wilfully,
Falsely, and knowing it was falsely done,
Publish upon a card, as Robert Southey's,
A face which might be just as like Tom Fool's,
Or John, or Richard Any-body-else's!
What had I done to thee, thou William Darton,
That thou shouldst for the lucre of base gain,
Yea, for the sake of filthy fourpences,
Palm on my countrymen that face for mine?
O William Darton, let the Yearly Meeting
Deal with thee for that falseness! All the rest
Are traceable; Smug's Hebrew family;
The German who might properly adorn
A gibbet or a wheel, and Monsieur Sooté,
Sons of Fitzbust the Evangelical;..
I recognize all these unlikenesses,
Spurious abominations tho' they be,
Each filiated on some original;
But thou, Friend Darton, and.. observe me, man,
Only in courtesy, and *quasi* Quaker,
I call thee Friend!.. hadst no original;
No likeness, or unlikeness, *silhouette*,
Outline, or plaister, representing me,
Whereon to form thy misrepresentation.
If I guess rightly at the pedigree
Of thy bad groatsworth, thou didst get a barber
To personate my injured Laureateship;
An advertising barber,.. one who keeps
A bear, and when he puts to death poor Bruin
Sells his grease, fresh as from the carcase cut,

Pro bono publico, the price per pound
Twelve shillings and no more. From such a barber,
O unfriend Darton! was that portrait made
I think, or peradventure from his block.

Next comes a minion worthy to be set
In a wooden frame; and here I might invoke
Avenging Nemesis, if I did not feel
Just now God Cynthius pluck me by the ear.
But, Allan, in what shape God Cynthius comes,
And wherefore he admonisheth me thus,
Nor thou nor I will tell the world; hereafter
The commentators, my Malones and Reids,
May if they can.   For in my gallery
Though there remaineth undescribed good store,
Yet " of enough enough, and now no more,"
(As honest old George Gascoigne said of yore,)
Save only a last couplet to express
That I am always truly yours,

R. S.*

Keswick, August, 1828.

* The main subject of this epistle having been suggested by
a poem of Bilderdijk's, part only of which I have incorpo-
rated, in a compressed and very inadequate translation, I
annex here the original, in justice to my deceased friend, — a
man of most extraordinary attainments, and genius not less
remarkable.

319

OP EENE VERZAMELING VAN MIJNE AFBEELDINGEN.

In pejus vultu proponi cereus usquam.—HORAT.

EEN Wildeman, het dolhuls uitgevlogen : [1]
  Een goede Hals, maar zonder ziel of kracht: [2]
Een Sukkelaar, die met verwonderde oogen
  Om alles met verbeten weêrzin lacht: [3]
Een Franschmans lach op halfverwrongen kaken,
  Die geest beduidt op 't aanzicht van een bloed: [4]
En, om 't getal dier fraaiheên vol te maken,
  Eens Financiers verwaande domme snoet. [5]
En dat moet ik, dat moet een Dichter wezen!
  Gelooft gy 't ooit, die deze monsters ziet?
Geeft, wat ik schreef, één trek daar van te lezen
  Zoo zeg gerust : " Hy kent zich zelven niet."

Maar zacht een poos!..Hoe langer hoe verkeerder!
  Men vormt my na uit Pottebakkers aard ; [6]
Doch de Adamskop beschaamt den kunstbootseerder,
  En 't zielloos ding is zelfs den klei niet waard...
Nu komt er een, die zal u 't echte leven
In lenig wasch met volle lijk'nis geven ;

[1] 1784.   [2] 1788.   [3] 1806.   [4] 1813.   [5] 1820.   [6] 1820.

En deze held, wat spreidt hy ons ten toon ?
De knorrigheid in eigen hoofdpersoon ;
Met zulk een lach van meêlij' op de lippen,
Als 't zelfgevoel eens Trotzaarts af laat glippen
Verachting spreidt op al wat hem omringt,
En half in spijt, zich tot verneedring dwingt. [1]

*   *   *   *   *   *

Mijn God ! is 't waar, zijn dit mijn wezenstrekken,
En is 't *mijn* hart, dat ze aan my-zelf onbdekken ?
Of maaldet gy, wier kunst my dus herteelt,
Uw eigen aart onwetend in mijn beeld ?
Het moog zoo zijn. De Rubens en Van Dijken
Zijn lang voorby, die zielen deên gelijken :
Wier oog hun ziel een heldre spiegel was,
En geest en hart in elken vezel las,
Niet, dagen lang, op 't uiterlijk bleef staren,
Maar d'eersten blik in 't harte kon bewaren,
Dien blik getrouw in klei of verven bracht,
En spreken deed tot Tijd-en-Nageslacht.

Die troffen, ja ! die wisten af te malen
    Wat oog en mond, wat elke zenuw sprak ;
Wier borst, doorstroomd van hooger idealen,
    Een hand bewoog die 't voorwerp noort, ontbrak.
Doch, wat maalt gy ? . . 't Misnoegen van 't vervelen
    Voor Rust der ziel in zalig zelfgenot ;
Met Ongeduld om 't haatlijk tijdontstelen ;
    En-Bitterheid, die met uw wanklap spot
Wen ge, om den mond iets vriendlijks af te pracnen,
    Of slaaprigheid of mijmrende ernst verstoort,

[1] 1822.

En door uw boert het aanzicht tergt tot lachen
Met zotterny, slechts wreevlig aangehoord.

Maar HODGES! gy, die uit vervlogen eeuwen
    De Schilderkunst te rug riept op 't paneel,
Geen mond mismaakt door 't zielverteerend geeuwen,
    Maar kunstgesprek vereenigt aan 't penceel!
Zoo 't Noodlot wil dat zich in later dagen
    Mijn naam bewaar in 't onwijs Vaderland,
En eenig beeld mijn leest moet overdragen,
    Het zij geschetst door uw begaafde hand.
In uw tafreel, bevredigd met my-zelven,
    Ontdek ik 't hart dat lof noch laster acht;
En, die daaruit mijn ziel weet op te delven
    Miskent in my noch inborst noch geslacht.*

1822.

* Rots-Galmen, d. ii. p. 103.

END OF THE THIRD VOLUME.

LONDON:
SPOTTISWOODES and SHAW,
New-street-Square.

www.ingramcontent.com/pod-product-compliance
Lightning Source LLC
Chambersburg PA
CBHW022208010726
47493CB00002B/466